WINNING
by MASTERING YOUR MIND

"Winning doesn't start around you it begins INSIDE you.
SO MAKE UP YOUR MIND!"

Mike Murdock

By Dr. Alan Pateman

BY DR. JENNIFER PATEMAN

AVAILABLE FROM APMI PUBLICATIONS, AMAZON.COM AND OTHER RETAIL OUTLETS

WINNING
by MASTERING YOUR MIND

DR. ALAN PATEMAN

BOOK TITLE:
WINNING by Mastering your Mind

WRITTEN BY Dr. ALAN PATEMAN
ISBN: 978-1-909132-40-5
eBook ISBN: 978-1-909132-55-9

Published By:
APMI Publications
In Partnership with Truth for the Journey Books **18**
Email: publications@alanpateman.com
www.AlanPatemanMinistries.com

Acknowledgements:
Author/Design/Senior Editor/Publisher: Apostle Dr. Alan Pateman
Editing/Proofreading/Research: Dr. Jennifer Pateman
Computer Administration/Office Manager: Dr. Dorothea Struhlik
Cover Image Credit: www.PosterMyWall.com

Unless otherwise indicated, Scripture quotations are from the King James Version of the bible.

*Where scriptures appear with special emphasis (**in bold,** italic or <u>underlined</u>) we have edited them ourselves in order to bring focused attention within the context of this subject being taught.*

❖

Dedication

To my administrator Doctor Dorothea Struhlik who is an ordained member of "Connecting for Excellence International Apostolic Network," on the Board of APMI as an Executive Elder and holds the position of Office Manager.

She is responsible for the daily management of my ministry office; assisting me in business administration, performance and student reviews etc.

Dorothea is also an Associate Professor and Board Member of LICU and has been so faithful in serving this ministry for the last 17 years.

❖

Table of Contents

❖

Introduction

Mind Games

I'd say you'll do best by filling your minds and meditating on things true, noble, reputable, authentic, compelling, gracious — the best, not the worst; the beautiful, not the ugly; things to praise, not things to curse (Philippians 4:8).

Every one of us have suffered at some point or another with mind games. So what are they? According to the dictionary, mind games are, "deliberate actions of calculated psychological manipulation intended to intimidate or confuse, usually for competitive advantage. Football players try to play mind games with the opposition; the jeweler's mind game is to convince lovers that the size of a gemstone reflects the depth of their feelings" (see http://www.thefree dictionary.com/mind+games).

All of us suffer with bombardments in the mind, none of us are immune. It certainly is a battlefield, but we must learn to be free, but how?

In today's society people are searching for mental liberty and if you buy the latest magazines, books or go online there is a plethora of articles focusing on the wellbeing of the mind. Just today I punched into my browser about the mind and instantly such titles spring up as:

- How to keep your mind off negative emotions *(such as negative films, news, relationships etc.!)*
- 30 ways to keep free of personal stress
- Identifying Mental Congestion
- Free Your Mind from Fear and Negative Emotional Baggage
- And so many more…!

I discovered that, **"Mental Health Awareness Week"** had already taken place *(January 16-20th, 2012)*. Surrounding that week were many different events and workshops catering for mental well-being. One site was offering *(amongst many other things):* **"Suicide prevention training"** as well as **"Stress and depression workshops."**

Basically there is a great awareness out there, not just amongst believers, that there is a dire need for mental fitness and that we need to address what we are filling our minds with on a daily basis and spend our time dwelling upon. Paul the apostle spoke very clearly in Philippians 4:7 that we should **"think on *these* things."**

Introduction

According to one particular article that I found online it says: "Your mental health is very important. **You will not have a healthy body if you don't also take care of your mind.**

People depend on you. It's important for you to take care of yourself so that you can do the important things in life — whether it's working, learning, taking care of your family, volunteering, enjoying the outdoors, or whatever is important to you."

It continues, "Good mental health helps you enjoy life and cope with problems. It offers a feeling of well being and inner strength. Just as you take care of your body by eating right and exercising, you can do things to protect your mental health. In fact, eating right and exercising can help maintain good mental health.

You don't automatically have good mental health just because you don't have mental health illness. You have to work to keep your mind healthy" (http://womenshealth. gov/mental-health/good-health).

Basically saying that we are what we eat, mentally as well as physically. This is not rocket science. Most of us know that consuming junk food will cause some long-term effects, yet we still do it. The same goes for the mind. If we are *heavy consumers* of mental rot, this too will have long-term effects. And yes most of us still continue to consume what we know to be unhealthy for our minds. Such as negative entertainment, negative reports on the news, music and all kinds of mentally disturbing things.

We tend to tell ourselves that we must "stay-in-the-know" otherwise we will become ignorant of the world around us. This not only defies logic when speaking of mental health, but also defies scripture, such as the one above that we already have read, Philippians 4:8.

My wife in her younger days attended Art College where her tutors were ruthlessly strict about what the students read. Anyone found with what was then considered a **"rubbish tabloid"** newspaper, were suspended without warning! They used this discipline to instill into the students, **"you are what you eat mentally!"**

They recognized that whatever influenced the creative juices of their students would reflect on them as a college. They were defending their own interests of course, because they held one of the best reputations in the country at that time.

All in all they helped the students grasp that if they were going to read newspapers at all, they needed to read *intelligent* ones! Needless to say this point of view did not necessarily do my wife any harm. It was generally good advice.

There's a lot to be said for common sense!

CHAPTER 1

Psychiatry & Psychology

Professions that Specialize

B e not conformed to this world: but be ye transformed by the renewing of your mind, that ye may prove what is that good, and acceptable, and perfect, will of God (Romans 12:2).

Psychiatry and Psychology are two professions that specialize on the Mind. <u>Psychiatry</u> is the medical specialty devoted to the study and treatment of mental disorders. <u>Psychology</u> is literally the **science of the mind**, which studies the mind's functions, especially those affecting *behaviour*. Considered by many, as an ***exact-science.***

However, they can only make such claims when studying *fallen-nature* because those who claim to be Christ's exhibit

His behaviour and way of thinking with their old natures and way of thinking passed away!

The word *psyche* comes from the ancient Greek for *soul;* what affects the mind directly affects the soul. Evidently we must exercise considerable vigilance when filtering what enters our minds and souls.

To make it clear how important this is we turn again to the same scripture that I used in the introduction. In each translation of the bible this particular passage reads slightly differently and all of them have their value. But this is particularly good:

> *Do not fret or have any anxiety about anything… and God's peace [shall be yours, that tranquil state of a soul assured of its salvation through Christ, and so fearing nothing from God and being content with its earthly lot of whatever sort that is, that peace] which transcends all understanding shall <u>garrison and mount guard over your hearts and minds</u> in Christ Jesus… <u>think on and weigh and take account of these things</u> [<u>fix your minds</u> on them] …and the God of peace (of untroubled, undisturbed well-being) will be with you.*
>
> *(Philippians 4:6-9 AMP)*

It's abundantly clear that it is OUR responsibility to purposefully think the right thoughts. To *"think on and weigh and take account of"* the right things. Only then, once we have done our part of the equation can we rely on the peace of God to *"garrison and mount guard over our hearts and minds in Christ Jesus."* This is not unlike the promise given us in the book of Isaiah where it says, *"Thou wilt keep him in perfect peace, whose mind is stayed on thee"* (26:3).

Better still is the Amplified Version: *"You will guard him and keep him in perfect and constant peace whose mind [both its inclination and its character] is stayed on You, because he commits himself to You, leans on You, and hopes confidently in You"* (Isaiah 26:3 AMP). Inclination and character can stand for behaviour and any number of things can influence our behaviour if we allow them to.

The Message Bible says it slightly different again: *"People with their minds set on you, you keep completely whole, steady on their feet, because they keep at it and don't quit"* (Isaiah 26:3 MSG).

That's an awesome promise. So simple and yet so hard, especially in the world today where more distractions exist than ever before with the invention of high tech gadgets, games and the Internet. All designed to crowd the right things OUT of our minds, not into them! Including God.

In High Demand

Psychology today is becoming more and more popular and not only in the secular world. Many Christians open to this science of human behaviour and employ it within their churches and ministries. From a secular point of view psychology is needed in many different jobs, such as the police force and many more. They have to know why people do what they do, in the world of criminality for instance.

Different dominant and submissive behaviours that help explain how individuals where motivated to do the things they do. This helps police with their investigations. They are dealing with the fallen nature expressed through crime all the time – so there is room for psychology but not at the expense of the Word of God.

Only when we begin to replace the truth of God's Word for behavioural science is there a problem and when we mix the two together! The danger is in the mixture. Keeping it separate keeps it safe!

Let me quote one particular source called the "Learnhub" who are promoting education and psychology in particular – here is what they have to say:

"You can use your knowledge of people to pursue a career in law, management or education. Help save the world by helping the needy through social work or fighting crime in criminology. **Psychology grads are in high demand everywhere"** (http://psychology.learnhub.com/lesson/3787-why-study-psychology).

"In High demand everywhere..." this should tell us something. People the world over are trying to be one step ahead. If they can understand what is behind behavioural patterns, then they have better chances of manipulating it for all sorts of reasons. Controlling behaviour or manipulation on a large scale is nothing new!

There is psychology in everything, from advertising on billboards about the latest films, to shopping for clothes in the high street and *large advertising companies desperately want to manipulate the minds of the masses to buy their product or brand.* So it stands to reason that they employ all the knowledge that they can about human behaviour. Just like it says in the quote above, psychology is *"…in high demand everywhere."*

This is where we come in. As Christians we are not to try and fix, manipulate or control our behaviour or anyone else's. Our old nature has passed away and all things have become new. We should not manipulate nor be easily led and manipulated anymore.

We stand for a different kind of freedom, from the contrived and manufactured control we see around us everyday. And not all control is negative. There must be order. But only in Christ can we have inner freedom and *remain* free of the influences of this world. The responsibility is all ours, "Pure religion and undefiled before God is this, …to *keep himself* unspotted from the world" (*James 1:27*).

> *Be not conformed to this world: but be <u>ye transformed by the renewing of your mind</u>, that ye may prove what is that good, and acceptable, and perfect, will of God.*
> (*Romans 12:2*)

Deliverance from Self-indulgence

When we get our minds off of ourselves – that's where true deliverance is! One sure fast way to stop our addiction to complaining is to visit the less fortunate *(esp. hospices).* In the natural there are things that we can do to modify our behaviour and keep ourselves in check. But *walking* by the Word and the power of the Holy Spirit is the way of the disciple.

Summary:

- We are only as strong as our spirit man
- We are what we eat – what are we feeding our soul?
- Obedience vs. disobedience
- Overcoming and making dreams a reality comes via obedience
- What are we thinking about?
- Is the mind stopping us moving into obedience?
- Victory is a process
- Line upon line – precept upon precept – walking out the Rhema Word
- Victory today prepares us for victory tomorrow
- Feed the mind with the right things - Philippians 4:6-9
- The importance of testimony
- The importance of vision
- Eliminate the worry: fix the mind on God
- Disciplined mind vs. a wondering mind
- If you are not free in your mind nor will the people around you be
- You will control the future... both yours and theirs

❖

CHAPTER 2

Happiness begins between your Ears

Tapping into Potential

Personally I enjoy watching people *succeed* in this life; excelling in their God given purpose; increasing in their knowledge of Him, as they continue walking in obedience. Yet I have witnessed many Christians who are incapacitated because they do not know how to protect their thought lives.

This one thing I do ... I press toward the mark...
(Philippians 3:13-14)

There's nothing more tragic than an unanswered call or untapped potential, this grieves the Spirit of God inside of me. Just how much does God enjoy watching over our individual growth and development!

In the same way that the artist treasures his painting or the master craftsman admires his craft, so too does our creator cherish us. He always has our best interests at heart; our dreams, goals, well-being and quality of life. All of which He intended for us to enjoy, so long as we live within the boundary of the mind of Christ.

The fact is this if we have the mind of Christ; we will adopt an excellent lifestyle; which is not for the weary! It is keenly developed on a daily basis incorporating our speech, thoughts and actions: spirit, soul and body. The collective meaning for the word conduct is: behaviour, manner, ways, carry out, accomplish, perform, demeanour.

Everyone develops THEIR OWN Set of values and Ethos

Every one of us by the time we reach our adulthood year has developed a personal set of values and ethos *(inner rules, codes of conduct, philosophies)*. According to the dictionary, *"ethos* characterizes the spirit of a culture, era, or community as manifested in its beliefs and aspirations."

Any *ethos (no matter how old or entrenched)* can be challenged or changed, but according to the dictionary *ethos* represents, the spirit, character, atmosphere, climate, mood, tenor, essence, disposition, rationale, morality, moral code, value system, principles, standards, ethics… and customs, that people erect individually and collectively, for a myriad of reasons.

For instance the experiences of our formative years really help to shape our emotional infrastructure, especially later on in life, with complex systems of self-defence. We enrol into the social club called, survival of the fittest and develop our own brand of insecurity.

Yet while we learn to survive we also learn to *self-destruct!* Once we meet Christ, however, all such inward complexities and psychologies have to alter forever! Meeting Him in reality causes eternal transformation and renewal.

The mind is a caldron pot of ideas, which develops its own shape *through generational, sociological and political influences, including basic family semantics!* It has all got to be *transformed* into a new shape and demeanour that spells *"Christ."* Clearly it is not possible to know Him and remain the same.

We discover that our floored systems of personal defence are totally *inadequate* and our sources of collective advice are completely bankrupt in comparison. Instead the realization of our total *necessity* for a Saviour meets us head-on; our need for Him to be *Lord and Master* to whom we can give final control. Allowing Him alone to shape our morals and ideas and navigate our inner compass! The answer can only be, **"the Word and the Spirit of God within us."**

As Christians we have the opportunity to be revolutionized and transformed inwardly upon knowing Christ. The evidence of which is to be substantiated through our outward behaviour and influence on the world and culture around us.

Regeneration is instant but renewal of the mind takes time. Sanctification is a lifelong process, a critical transition involving the continual laying off the carnal mind and taking on *(learning to yield to)* the Mind of Christ; *sanctification is to be set apart and made holy.* Our minds are intended for holy use, and should not *"wonder out of the presence of God."* Something quite hard to achieve in this day and age, but with the fruit of self control it can be done!

Renewal is a lengthy process, requiring much more than isolated efforts of bible study! It takes dedicated self-adjustment learning to think like Christ!

Mind Management

Many Christians are incapacitated because they do not know how to protect their own thought lives. Satan will bombard us with confusion, fear, hatred, suspicion, depression, mistrust and a host of other mental distractions.

Someone once said, *"Happiness begins between your ears and your mind is the drawing room for tomorrow's circumstances..."*

Remember, what happens in your mind will happen in time and therefore one of our first priorities must be *mind-management.*

❖

Chapter 3

Worry is Practical Atheism!

The Definition of a Pessimist & Cynic

We have all experienced friends or colleagues who have had a pessimistic nature and who loved to dampen the zeal of those around them, with their endless humanistic arguments *(cynicism)*. Perhaps even experienced an employee who always liked to point out the negatives and reasons why things can't be done the way that they have been planned.

Lord, I believe; help thou mine unbelief.

(Mark 9:24)

They draw attention to every possible obstacle, instead of just remaining positive and getting on with the job that they have been asked to do!

Pessimists always poison the atmosphere of hope. We must guard against this for the sake of everyone else involved.

The definition of a pessimist is someone who is *"gloomy and distrustful."* While the definition of a cynic is someone who *"scoffs and is always suspicious, dubious and sceptical."* Such characters are only willing to KNOW EVERYTHING AND BELIEVE NOTHING. Their attitude towards everyone and everything is that of complete *"indifference."* In other words their talent is to coldly trivialize and demean *everything!* **The only thing that impresses them is the force of their own mind!**

I would suggest that many people are cynics at heart and privately scoff at the simplicity of faith. Such people take zero risks for themselves but instead like to spend energy analysing the behaviour of those who do. They are a contradiction to themselves and don't realise it.

The Pragmatist

In today's world *"pragmatism"* is deemed a commendable quality because it is cold towards the dynamics of faith. It could be said like this: pragmatism is generally where *all-things-practical* start and *all-things-spiritual* stop.

When it comes to believers who still value their pragmatic roots *(upbringing),* they usually have a tendency to be overly practical and see the spiritual experiences of others as *excess.* Their security tends to be in their own set of scruples. Scripture however is very clear about this: ***"Do not rely on your own insight or understanding..."*** *(Proverbs 3:5 AMP)*

*Trust God from the bottom of your heart; **don't try to figure out everything on your own.** Listen for God's voice in everything you do, everywhere you go; he's the one who will keep you on track. **Don't assume that you know it all.** Run to God! Run from evil! Your body will glow with health, your very bones will vibrate with life! Honour God with everything...*

(Proverbs 3:5-7 MSG)

The Humanist

Today we are moving into a new threshold - where the tree of knowledge is worshiped on a level more than at any other time in history. Knowledge represents power, wealth and opportunity – so there is an all-out lust for it across the earth.

It's not all negative of course, unless you include the fact that the age for Sex Education has dropped to kindergarten age! There is a time for everything. Even knowledge! But we all live in *a-need-to-know* generation; a time in history where the internet is *breeding* untold realities.

Therefore another character we often find ourselves rowing the boat with is the chronic humanist! These are the ones who want to *reason-everything-out* from a human standpoint and reject the importance of faith in Deity.

They always look for the problems and all the reasons why faith can't work! They magnify the problems above the solutions and drain all mental, physical and spiritual energy from those around them. Like the pragmatist, they have a knack for dampening the enthusiasm and inspiration of others while at the same time appearing to support it.

The confusion develops due to their *"mixture."* On one hand they want the benefits that are reaped from a life of faith, but simultaneously and openly mock the simplicity of faith. They are incapable of paying any price or offering themselves in surrender. Their endless interrogations are mind-boggling; they seduce and are themselves easily seduced through sophistication and complicated disputes.

However with their typical *"heady"* approach to everything, they tire easily. Exhausting themselves due to **over-thinking** (*this type of person is not always a high-achiever!*) As a team member or employee they can exasperate everybody else! Much time is spent trying to keep them buoyant, motivated and *"up."* With all their *"talk"* and endless chatter, they tend to be very entertaining but largely unreliable. Whenever left to their own devices, they usually manage to talk themselves out of a job *and this would describe the average believer!*

The Worrier

Another undesirable character is that of worry, being over concerned, troubled, fretful and anxious. It is a bible sin! Especially prevalent right now when confidence in the global economy is zilch! Nevertheless the bible never retreats and warns us not to cast away our confidence, guaranteeing *recompense* to those who don't lose heart.

> Cast not away therefore your CONFIDENCE, which hath great recompense of reward.
>
> *(Hebrews 10:35)*

*CONFIDENCE (Strong's #G3954): parrhesia par-rhay-see'-ah from #G3956 and a derivative of #G4483; **all out-spokenness,** i.e. frankness, bluntness, publicity; by implication, **assurance:--bold** (X -ly, -ness, -ness **of speech**), confidence, X freely, X openly, X plainly(-ness). See #G3956 and #G4483.*

Interestingly biblical CONFIDENCE as mentioned here, involves *"ALL OUT-SPOKENNESS AND BOLD-NESS OF SPEECH!"* Perhaps it's much easier for us to imagine ourselves as being confident, within the confines of our own minds, but true CONFIDENCE is not concealed – it is revealed - through our *"speech."*

Unbelief & Realism

I quote Pastor John Hagee when I say, **"Worry is practical atheism"** *(applied-unbelief!)* Atheism by definition means: *"...disbelief in or denial of the existence of God or gods."* And when we worry or lend too much thinking to the flesh, this is literally *"denying God."* We are all capable of this on a daily basis, especially in challenging situations. That's when many of us found out what we are really made of.

Many *"believers"* define themselves by their own behaviour, as *"non-believers."* Selah! For this we must admire the individual in the bible who spoke so honestly to Jesus, *"Lord, I believe; help thou mine unbelief"* (Mark 9:24). To avoid the temptation of ever covering up our own unbelief, we must adopt the same simple prayer!

He that overcometh shall inherit all things; and I will be his God, and he shall be my son. BUT THE FEARFUL AND

UNBELIEVING, *and the abominable, and murderers, and whoremongers, and sorcerers, and idolaters, and all liars, shall have their part in the lake, which burneth with fire and brimstone: which is the second death.*

(Revelation 21:7-8)

I've heard some believers mistakenly call themselves *"realists"* intending to mean they don't pretend or mince-words, but *"say-things-for-what-they-really-are."* However such self-appointed realism can often *(insensitively)* be dished-out at the *expense* of others. I would even say at the expense of faith, when faith is erroneously replaced for realism in an attempt to be seen as non-religious.

God chose us to please Him by faith alone and not by being heady! There is room for being a doer and pro-active. But people, who have given themselves to a legitimate walk of faith in Christ, have to learn not to depend on their rationality or the *"arm of the flesh."*

With him is an arm of flesh; but with us is the LORD our God to help us, and to fight our battles. And the people rested themselves *upon the words of Hezekiah king of Judah.*

(2 Chronicles 32:8)

Remember everything that God has ever done or will ever do, is controversial! Those of us therefore, who heavily depend on our own reasoning, will miss God every time! Either we *see* things as the flesh reveals them or as God reveals them. To be IN CHRIST we must be seers by His Spirit alone and not by our own instincts.

Note: (this is not always negative by the way and the prophetic ministry must be known for more than its ability to point out all of the negatives!)

Learn how to Insulate!

A piece of free advice that I would heartily give to anyone who asks is this: *choose* very carefully who you have working closely around you. However if such a choice does *not* belong to us, then the only alternative we have is to learn to insulate!

People in close proximity on a daily basis can display the characteristics that we have been discussing here: chronic unbelief, worry, strong-willed-pragmatism and inexhaustible humanism – all of which oppose our faith. Such people always make it a slog and test our agility in God.

Faith believes for the best to happen but they always look for the negatives. They busy themselves working-everything-out. Calculating all of the impossibilities before your faith has had chance to exercise.

Usually those operating in such behaviour suffer with rejection and don't have a true revelation of who *they* are in Christ *(they still operate from an orphan spirit)*. However those who truly WALK WITH CHRIST on a daily basis – simply don't worry any longer. Instead they have learnt that for Jesus to be the ANSWER, nothing else can be the problem! That if He says, "Yes" there is no one standing who can say "No!"

The Lord Hath Seen

Our heavenly Father will take care of every issue that concerns our lives; He is more aware of the things that we need than we are. To prove this all we have to do is turn to the Word where we find the very names of God revealed. One of the numerous names that the scriptures apply to God is *"Jehovah Jireh."* Many know this to mean: The Lord provides. But it can also be understood as: *"The Lord hath seen."*

And Abraham called the name of that place Jehovah–jireh: as it is said to this day, In the mount of the LORD it shall be seen.

(Genesis 22:14)

And he called the name of that place, The Lord seeth. Whereupon even to this day it is said: In the mountain the Lord will see.

(Genesis 22:14 DRA)

Jehovah–jireh (Strong's #H3070):
*Yhovah yireh yeh-ho-vaw' yir-eh' from #H3068 and #H7200; **Jehovah will see (to it);** Jehovah-Jireh, a symbolical name for Mount Moriah:--Jehovah- jireh. See #H3068 and #H7200.*

Even though the above scripture has many implications, we can safely say, in this particular context, that NOTHING SLIPS THE GOD RADAR! He sees what's needed before we do – past, present and future. In fact every provision has all ready been made and all we must do is apply our faith and make steady withdrawals on our heavenly account.

Everything that the Father achieved through sending His Son - is still at our disposal. Therefore we have the immense security of knowing that nothing NEW can ever be brought to God's attention, He is always way ahead of us!

An important point to add here is that God is not only ABLE to meet our needs but He is always WILLING to meet our needs. We could say it like this: GOD IS JUST AS WILLING AS HE IS ABLE. Sadly however most people don't believe this fact. When asked whether God is ABLE, the response is usually positive. But when it comes to whether God is WILLING or not – the response is usually mixed or negative.

This is influenced of course by the fact that many of us have the inherent belief that somehow we are not good enough or that our mistakes have hindered God somehow. Thankfully the provisions of God *(His Son and all else besides)* were never based on our perfection but on HIS!

❖

CHAPTER 4

Destiny in our Mouths

God doesn't ACT without "Saying" it First

Faith operates through believing and saying... and saying... and saying! Only our words of faith can bring about possession. This is not just theory but fact. As Charles Capps says, *"It is spiritual law... that works every time it is applied correctly."* GOD NEVER DOES ANYTHING WITHOUT SAYING IT FIRST.

Out of the abundance of the heart the mouth speaketh...
(Matthew 12:34-35)

He is a faith God who releases His faith through His Words. *"Jesus answering saith unto them, Have faith in God"* (Mark 11:22). A more literal translation of that verse would say, *"Have the God kind of faith"* or *"the faith of God."*

Ephesians 5:1 literally tells us to be imitators of God as children imitate their parents. Likewise in order to imitate God we must talk like Him and act like Him. Jesus Himself operated in the faith principles of Mark 11:23, and Matthew 17:20 while He was on earth. He spoke to the wind and sea. He spoke to demons. He spoke to the fig tree. He even spoke to dead men! They obeyed His SPOKEN WORDS, which had power and influence.

Obviously the key here is all about words of faith that are SPOKEN. Jesus did not "metallize" the elements nor the demons! He *spoke* to them. We too must verbalize our faith. As the scripture below clearly states… we are the Lord's redeemed and we certainly have much to "SAY."

Let the redeemed of the Lord SAY so, *whom he hath redeemed from the hand of the enemy.*

(Psalm 107:2)

IMITATION that Gets the Same Results

Jesus operated in the God kind of faith; God is a faith God. He released faith through His Words and we must follow suit. Instead of speaking words loaded with fear and doubt, we must speak words of faith. Instead of speaking words of negativity and death, we must speak words of life *(see Genesis 1:3).*

Jesus imitated His heavenly Father and got the same results! The same applies to us and in John 14:12 Jesus said, *"He that believeth on me the works that I do shall he do also; and greater..."* Such principles of faith are based on spiritual laws that work for *whosoever* applies them and sets them into motion.

However we must honestly ask ourselves, *"Do I really want all the negative things that I have been speaking to come to pass?"* Absolutely not! Yet if God spoke to each of us today and said, *"From this day forth everything you say, will happen exactly as you said it;"* our vocabulary would be drastically altered forever!

Words Produce what they Contain

Spoken words program our spirit *(heart)* either towards success or defeat. **Words are truly containers; carrying and producing whatever they contain;** *"...faith cometh by hearing and hearing by the Word of God" (Romans 10:17).* Faith comes more quickly when we hear ourselves quoting, speaking, and saying the same things God says. We will more readily receive God's Word into our spirits by hearing ourselves speaking it... than if we hear someone else speaking it.

Much of what the Father supplies to the Body of Christ is furnished through our confession. This is not simply our positive, premeditated confession expressed in prayer; it consists of *everything* that comes out of our mouths. *"But I tell you, on the day of judgment men will have to give account for every idle (inoperative, nonworking) word they speak" (Matthew 12:36 AMP).* Yikes!

The International Standard Bible Encyclopaedia (ISBE) states:

The Greek word (argós) generally used for "idle or idleness" in the New Testament literally meant: inactive, useless, empty gossip, nonsensical talk. Whereas the Strong's Concordance #G692 takes argos (pronounced ar-gos') as generally meaning: inactive, unemployed; lazy, useless; barren, idle or slow.

Negative words that we include into our daily banter, vernacular, relaxed chatter and individual vocabulary, can appear so harmless, yet prove so reckless. Therefore making a determined effort to alter our day-to-day jargon, is one of the best ways that we can offer ourselves a better future and lifestyle, while simultaneously having a healthier influence upon the lives of others.

Such a modest adjustment perhaps, but anyone who has ever tried, will know just how hard it really is to tame this rogue organ called the tongue! The more we try, very often the worse things become. All of which is brought into sharp focus with this following scripture:

We all often stumble and fall and offend in many things. And if anyone does not offend in speech [never says the wrong things], he is a fully developed character and a perfect man, able to control his whole body and to curb his entire nature.

If we set bits in the horses' mouths to make them obey us, we can turn their whole bodies about. Likewise, look at the ships: though they are so great and are driven by rough winds, they are steered by a very small rudder wherever the impulse of the helmsman determines.

*Even so the tongue is a little member, and it can boast of great things. See how much wood or how great a forest a tiny spark can set ablaze! **And the tongue is a fire. [The tongue is a] world of wickedness set among our members, contaminating and depraving the whole body and setting on fire the wheel of birth (the cycle of man's nature), being itself ignited by hell (Gehenna).***

*For every kind of beast and bird, of reptile and sea animal can be tamed and has been tamed by human genius (nature). **But the human tongue can be tamed by no man. It is a restless (undisciplined, irreconcilable) evil, full of deadly poison.***

*With it we bless the Lord and Father, and with it we curse men who are made in God's likeness! **Out of the same mouth come forth blessing and cursing…. Does a fountain send forth [simultaneously] from the same opening fresh water and bitter?** …Neither can a salt spring furnish fresh water.*

(James 3:1-12 AMP)

The Message Bible says, *"You're not going to dip into a polluted mud hole and get a cup of clear, cool water, are you?"* (verse 12)

Romans chapter 7 also reveals the sharp contrast of a life struggling with the flesh, compared to a life that has been surrendered to the governing guidance of God's Holy Spirit. Our old nature is what gives Satan access or a foothold in our lives. If allowed, he will fight every progress that we ever make, therefore we *must* "put it off" for good. Even then it will seek resurrection to project and leak its ideas and proposals. The only solution then is to give ZERO opportunity to the flesh or to the devil, as scripture warns:

> *Leave no [such] room or foothold for the devil [give* no *opportunity to him].*
>
> *(Ephesians 4:27 AMP)*

The Creative Force of Almighty God

In Hebrews 3:1 we are instructed to "*...consider the Apostle and High Priest of our profession, Christ Jesus.*" The word translated as *"profession"* in this verse can also be translated as *"confession."* God appointed and anointed Jesus to be High Priest over our confessions or our words of faith.

1 Corinthians 1:4-5 also tells us that Jesus enriches our utterance. That is, He takes our words of faith and enriches them with His anointing. So no matter how we look at it, **the words we speak can carry the very creative force of almighty God behind them. When that is the case, they WILL come to pass!**

Prophets of Our Own Lives

God created us to be the prophets of our own lives! Our destinies are within reach, even in our own mouths! It is OUR words, which determine the final course of our lives, success or failure. We need to be speaking the right thing, we have no excuse: "The word is nigh thee, even in they mouth, and in thy heart: that is, the world of faith..." *(Romans 10:8-9)*

The word that saves is right here, as near as the tongue in your mouth, as close as the heart in your chest. It's the word of faith that welcomes God to go to work and set things right for us.

(Romans 10:8-9 MSG)

Our words bring either good or evil things to pass in our lives. **So there is no other option than to take responsibility for every single word that leaves our lips.** It's tempting to dismiss this fact, particularly when we're in a mood to rant or vent! But no amount of *indifference* will alter TRUTH on this matter. In addition our words will link us to consequences, which develop as a direct result of something careless we said.

This is very similar to DNA evidence in a court case that links a criminal to his crime. So too will our words hold us ever responsible *(Selah!)* This is a *"no-brainer" (something that "requires little mental effort!")* To guard our speech is the smartest move we can ever make, to ensure the quality of life around us.

In other words, it's in our own best interest and that of others to use our mouths to bless and not to curse. Nevertheless our fountains must be kept clean, they cannot flow with *mixture* - both salt water and fresh! *(Matthew 12:34-37)*

The result of speaking words of life around people is that we create an *"appetite"* in them that wants to "live-up-to" our positive expectations, rather than bringing them low with oppressive negativity.

Four New Testament Confessions

Let's take a look at four basic kinds of confession that can be found throughout the New Testament.

The First Confession: REPENTANCE

The first confession found in the New Testament is the confession of sin taught by John the Baptist and Jesus to the Jewish people in their day. This act of confession however, is NOT what we know today as Christian repentance. Actually, the confession of sin and water baptism that we read about in Matthew 3 and Luke 3 was an act by the people of Israel under the Abrahamic *(or Old)* Covenant.

Prior to Jesus going to the cross, the Jews knew what it was to confess their sins and repent, but their sins were only "covered" in atonement by the blood of an animal, which was sacrificed once a year. It wasn't until the sacrifice of Jesus' blood that sin could actually be wiped out and not just covered up *(see Hebrews 10)*.

The Second Confession: SALVATION

The second confession described in the New Testament applies to everyone, the confession of a sinner. **It's what we now know as the prayer of salvation.** In John 16, when Jesus told His disciples about the soon coming Holy Spirit, He explained that the Spirit would come to convict *"the world"* of sin. But what were these *"sinners"* to do, once convicted by the Spirit? Basically, the confession of a sinner under the New Covenant is simply, "JESUS IS LORD."

The word is nigh thee, even in thy mouth, and in thy heart: that is, the word of faith, which we preach; that if thou shalt confess with thy mouth the Lord Jesus, and shalt believe in thine heart that God hath raised Him from the dead, thou shalt be saved.

(Romans 10:8-9)

Third Confession: SIN

Today the Church is full of Christians who have no idea how to confess their sins once they do step out of fellowship with the Father - which is our third New Testament confession. The bible says if we have sin in our lives, we must get it out - confess it, repent of it, get rid of it. Once we do this, we must stand on 1 John 1:9, which says, *"If we confess our sins, he is faithful and just to forgive us our sins, and to cleanse us from all unrighteousness."*

According to 1 John 1- 2 when we are out of fellowship with the Father, when we sin - we know it. That's the time to get rid of it. Immediately! After all, 1 John 2:1 assures us that, *"If any man sin, we have an advocate with the Father, Jesus Christ the righteous."* We must not run from Him when we sin, but to Him. The moment we confess our sin is the moment we get rid of it. By faith, we spew it out of our mouths and God is faithful and just to *"forgive"* and to *"cleanse."*

The Fourth Confession: FAITH

This fourth and final confession found in the New Testament is the confession of our faith in God's Word, our faith in Christ, our faith in God the Father, and our faith in the faithfulness of Jesus as our High Priest. We must remember *whatever* we receive from God, we receive it by CONFESSION. Our mouths are our **"Master Key to Life!"** Again the Apostle Paul wrote to the Hebrews: *"...consider the Apostle and High Priest of our confession Christ Jesus" (Hebrews 3:1 NASB).*

Saying The Same As God Says

To take a closer look, the word *"confession"* in the Greek actually means, *"saying the same thing as; saying what God says."* It's an affirmation of a bible truth we are particularly embracing, *(or)* repeating with our lips, the thing God has said in His Word, which we believe with our heart. We could say it like this: if we are mindful of the natural, we will live in the world, but if we are mindful of the Lord, we will live by faith.

From the fruit of his lips a man enjoys good things, but the unfaithful have a craving for violence. He who guards his lips guards his life, but he who speaks rashly will come to ruin.

(Proverbs 13:2-3 NIV)

The Amplified says, *"He who opens wide his lips comes to ruin"* and the Message Bible says; ***"The good acquire a*** *taste for helpful conversation; bullies push and shove their way through life. Careful words make for a careful life; **careless talk may ruin everything.**"*

Our confessions - the words we constantly speak day after day - determine what we receive from God, whether it's salvation, physical healing, peace or financial prosperity. What's more, for the rest of our eternal existence, this principle of faith working hand in hand with our confession will never change. Jesus told His disciples in Mark 11:22; *"Have faith in God."* or, as one translation puts it, *"Have the faith of God."* In verse 23, He went on to explain how that faith process works:

> *Whosoever shall say unto this mountain, be thou removed, and be thou cast into the sea; and shall not doubt in his heart, but shall believe that those things which he saith shall come to pass; he shall have whatsoever he saith.*
>
> *(Mark 11:23)*

Faith Relentlessly Speaks What it Believes

It is our confession or words of faith that bring possession. We see this in Romans 10:10 *"With the heart man believeth...and with the mouth confession is made..."* And in Matthew 12:34-35, *"Out of the abundance of the heart the mouth speaketh..."*

We lay hold of the Word by receiving it by faith and then CONFESSING it *(confession brings possession)*. The same process that's involved in our salvation experience is necessary for everything else we will ever receive from God *(that is already promised to us)*. Remember, once we lay hold of the promises of God with our faith and our confession, that's when Jesus' enriching anointing and ministry come into play. That's why the Apostle Paul taught Timothy about being *"...nourished up in the words of faith"* rather than *"old wives fables" (1 Timothy 4:6-7).*

Nourished on Words OF Faith

Literally then words of faith **"nourish"** while idle and poorly chosen words don't. Simply by definition, that which is mal-nourished *(or under-nourished)* is actually "half-starved!" So in summary, when we choose not to focus on the nourishing words of faith, but choose idle nonsense instead, we are literally limiting, starving and bringing weakness to our own spirits.

This concept of spiritual self-nourishing is also seen here in the Amplified Version:

If you lay all these instructions before the brethren, you will be a worthy steward and a good minister of Christ Jesus, ***EVER NOURISHING YOUR OWN SELF ON THE TRUTHS OF THE FAITH*** *and of the good [Christian] instruction which you have closely followed. But* ***refuse and avoid irreverent legends (profane and impure and godless fictions, mere grandmothers tales) and silly myths...***

Train yourself toward godliness (piety), [keeping yourself spiritually fit]. For physical training is of some value (useful for a little), but godliness (spiritual training) is useful and of value in everything and in every way, for it holds promise for the present life and also for the life which is to come. This saying is reliable and worthy of complete acceptance by everybody.

(1 Timothy 4:6-9 AMP)

This gives us even more reason to obey what we read in Hebrews 10:23, where it clearly instructs us to, "Hold fast the profession of our faith..." which can make the difference between life and death.

Once having nourished ourselves rightly on the Word of God, we have three fundamental steps to take, in regards to activating the promises of God in our lives:

- We must Ask According to His Word
- We must Act on our Faith in His Word
- We must Praise Him in Response to His Word

❖

CHAPTER 5

Our God Given Antidote to Stress

Avoiding Self-Destruction

Stress is such a successful tool for the devil because once he can get us to engage with stress; we self-destruct!

But the fruit of the Spirit is love, joy, peace, longsuffering, gentleness, goodness, faith, meekness, temperance: against such there is no law.

(Galatians 5:22-23)

Today I was on my instant messenger and up popped an advert with a slim fast product *(a fat burning pill that promised results in just one week!)* with the usual clever marketing, various tributes and a doctor to legitimize the product...!

Admittedly it was all very tempting to believe; nonetheless all *"short cuts"* make me dubious. Why? Because they usually don't work long term! Even something as important as salvation you can't jump the fence! *(Luke 13:24)*

As far as weight loss is concerned only the right kind of lifestyle that beats stress can also conquer the waistline! As experts say that the liver produces fat when under stress; proving the point that no amount of expensive creams, pills or other products can change us outwardly when the change we need is inward.

Even *scientifically proven* products are a waste if we are stressed out all the time. Stress will still increase those signs of aging no matter how much you spend on that cream! And while every effort *should* be made to improve our lives; without proper inward adjustments, all outward adjustments are sure to be counter-productive!

Addicted to the Feel-Good-Factor

This opens up a much deeper topic: the feel good factor. There are many people out there trying to be the next world famous feel-good-guru. Yet quality of life is important and that sense of genuine *well-being...* After all we *are* meant to live life more abundantly and it is the *good news* that we are advocating and not the bad! But consider how thin the line is, that exists between the feel good factor and compromising the gospel altogether!

If global persecution towards Christianity hit tomorrow, will we be amongst those who *"love not their lives unto death" (see Revelation 12:11)* or will we side with the popular notion; *"well this just does not make me feeeeel good; if I'm not happy doing it then I am just not going to do it!"* How far will we take this feel good gospel without undermining the whole plan of salvation? And while every soldier who signs up has the opportunity to die, can he enjoy life in-between? That's the question!

What's more you don't have to be molested as a child to be stressed out as an adult *(forgive the stark analogy...)* in fact the average person today is stressed out and we all have different reasons for being so! Whole congregations today admit to being stressed out.

It's an epidemic! But as Christians we should never be stressed out, nevertheless stress is such a successful tool for the devil because once he can get us to engage with stress; we *self-destruct!* In reality he needs to do very little while we do the rest. Little effort... big results...! Practically the entire Body of Christ live under stress making us unproductive for Christ and ineffective in our witness.

Fruitful Victory!

What remedies this current paradox better for the Christian other than the *fruits of the spirit? (see Galatians 5:22)* **Our best antidote is to seek first the Kingdom of God which is "...*righteousness, peace and joy in the Holy Spirit"* (see *Matthew 6:33, Romans 14:17).*

Basically, **stress free living is the result of living by the Spirit** "...against such there is no law" (see *Galatians 5:23).*

His burden is light and His yoke is easy and His joy is our strength... *(see Matthew 11:30; Nehemiah 8:10)*

Are we confused with inspirational speaking versus preaching? It is true that while we must encourage people to live life to the fullest and be happy, we must not *sell-out or compromise* the gospel in the process! And while precious people this world-over are dying for the sake of the gospel, there are others who just want to *"feel good"* about it! *Do we really want to be that shallow?*

How's it Working for You?

The ultimate question is this: *"What has Christianity really done for us?"* If we are not living an overcoming life, then what does being a Christian actually mean? When we overcome in this life, it provides the world around us with the evidence that we are actually walking with God. No matter how hard it gets, we just keep going.

> *Ye are of God, little children, and have overcome them: because greater is he that is in you, than he that is in the world.*
>
> *(1 John 4:4)*

The provision of the fruits in our lives not only allows us to walk in God's divine nature, but also empower us, to walk by His Spirit on a day-to-day basis. Relying less upon ourselves and more upon Him means that we are less likely to succumb to the pressures of the world around us.

The facts are plain: the Holy Spirit achieves more in our lives than just speaking in religious tongues. In fact every religion has its own brand of weirdness along with its own unique mantra. Yet we better treat the Holy Spirit with more dignity and respect than just another source of mantra!

❖

CHAPTER 6

The Cancer of Chaos & Spiritual Anarchy

Free or just out of Control?

Have you ever considered why cancer is such a threat in today's world? Why are so many people suffering with this unsolvable problem? With today's technology the way that it is, cancer still seems to defy even the best minds. What is the cause, what is the cure?

Listening to Dr Don Colbert and Brother Copeland discussing this subject I heard the simplest definition for cancer that I've heard yet. They simply approached the subject of cancer as being the end result of **"...cells rebelling against the body!"** Basically meaning that cancer is the result of rebellion that manifests in the body, at cell level. Rogue cells attacking the body like a bunch of lawless thugs and breaking down the body's immune system.

There can be several reasons for this unhealthy living, thinking and attitudes. Sowing seeds of rebellion over time certainly will produce a harvest. This is one thing that we can be certain of! We must be watchful over the type of seeds that we sow.

> Be not deceived; God is not mocked: for <u>whatsoever</u> a man soweth, that shall he also reap.
>
> (Galatians 6:7)

> That is why many of you are weak and sick and some have even died. But if we would examine ourselves, we would not be judged by God in this way. Yet when we are judged by the Lord, we are being disciplined so that we will not be condemned along with the world.
>
> (1 Corinthians 11:30-32 NLT; see also AMP)

However to encourage balance here I must say that not all sick people, *(whether from cancer or otherwise)*, are guilty of rebellion! We must be careful not to adopt condemning theologies. I had a certain friend some years ago who was very dear to my wife and I... but I found out the hard way one day what his theology truly consisted of.

Gallstones or Sin!

I had spent five hours reeling with pain while passing gall stones from my bladder... perhaps it was the nearest experience to giving birth for a male! I was rushed to an

Italian hospital late at night, to have my kidneys scanned and to be seen by specialists... but when I spoke with my dear friend by phone to ask for prayer, and besides other harsh opinions he mainly implied, *"maybe you are in sin?"* That day I discovered what Job must have felt like!

O'boy, I was truly shocked and it occurred to me then, that people only lose that kind of harsh theology when they themselves are sick! On the other hand sin *can* be a factor in sickness but not *always* and we must safe guard ourselves from adopting theologies that are either "all inclusive and compromising" or "condemning and judgmental." They are equally as bad!

If you have ever passed gallstones then you'll know just how painful that was for me! I was literally on my knees for five long hours begging God; like all of us do, when in a fix we can't control! You bet the first thing I did was check my heart! But in the end it just turned out to be, too many years of drinking too much strong English tea and drinking too little water! I've changed my lifestyle a little since then!

There are all kinds of reasons for thinking the way that we do... many times our own experiences dictate to us... and if we are hard on ourselves, then we are likely to be hard on others too. My friend was less than understanding and sadly his theology was very condemning.

So having been on the receiving end of that, I certainly don't want to dish out any condemnation on the sick... but having said that, **there has to be real weight to the Word of God. If everything can be just explained away, then it has**

little value to it. Cancer is spiritual but eventually manifests itself in the flesh. Even our churches suffer from spiritual rebellion, cancers... in fact I dare say that the Body of Christ is riddled with it! Metaphorically speaking...!

A Cultural Blend of Rebellion

So many people have no respect for authority or even godly order... whether in secular life or in Christendom. They walk out of jobs the minute they don't like something or file out of churches the minute they don't agree! This amounts to a cultural blend of rebellion. And as a result a harvest of rebellion is being reaped upon entire generations of people. People are afraid of cancer mainly because they can't control it... but neither can you control a rebellious heart.

We have to make sure that we are not stubborn and rebellious; the harvest on that type of seed is not the type of harvest we want!

The human heart is the most deceitful of all things, and desperately wicked. Who really knows how bad it is? But I, the LORD, search all hearts and examine secret motives. I give all people their due rewards, according to what their actions deserve.

(Jeremiah 17:9-10 NLT)

There is order in the body as God created it but cancerous cells rebel against that order, wreaking havoc in the body, breaking it down, a house that is divided against itself eventually falls. Being rebellious is synonymous with wanting our own way - rather than, "not my will Father but yours..." Instead we want to be in control of our own lives yet the harvest from that will be just as hard to control! In fact most people, who claim to be free, are actually *OUT OF CONTROL!*

❖

CHAPTER 7

The Winner's Mind

The Winner's Life

Ilove to see people succeed in life, just like the artist treasures his painting and the craftsman his violin, so our Creator cherishes His design! He is concerned about our dreams, goals and our ability to be happy and to enjoy life. But all said and done, none of us can truly enjoy life unless we STAY IN OUR RIGHT MINDS!

For as he thinketh in his heart, so is he...

(Proverbs 23:7)

Success is being happy. Happiness is basically feeling good about our lives and our plans. Two forces are vital to happiness: our relationships and our achievements. The gospel also has two forces: the Person of Jesus Christ, and the principles He taught. One is the Son of God; the other is the system of God.

One is the life of God; the other is the law of God. One is the King; the other is the Kingdom. One is an experience with God; the other is the expertise of God. One is heart-related the other is mind-related. Salvation is experienced *"instantaneously"* while God's wisdom principles are learned *"progressively,"* and both are essential for success and happiness.

A Living Priority

In everything therefore we must make it a priority to protect our thought lives. Some folks like to shout about their double portion but have never dealt with their fanatic in the attic! In reality the same Holy Spirit will make us deal with this chief opponent *first*.

There is no uncertainty about it, we must conquer our minds, and this is a place where there can be no demilitarized zone, no middle ground. Either it belongs to the enemy or to God.

When it comes to the mind there is no grey fudge. It is black or white, all or nothing. Another thing is for certain; where there is no discipline there is no Holy Spirit! He is never chaos. He is always order! Anyone who is successful today *(whether secular or Christian)* is someone who has mastered his or her minds with sheer "discipline." From businessmen to politicians, sports personnel or record breakers; they set their "minds" on a goal and don't deviate.

Sadly in retrospect many are incapacitated *(out of action!)* because they have never learnt how to protect their thought lives. Satan bombards them with fear, hatred, suspicion depression, mistrust and a host of other mental distractions *(or should I say "disorders!")* But why does this zone have to be the most vulnerable area of our lives?

Because happiness really does begin between our ears! The mind is the drawing room for tomorrow's successes or failures; what happens there *(in our minds)* happens in time. As scripture clearly tells us *"...as he thinketh in his heart, so is he" (Proverbs 23:7)*. So what you keep in mind from day to day is really what is shaping your future - positive or negative!

Making mind-management a MUST for any believer who seeks to be an over-comer! In fact it's not hard to recognise an over-comer from an defeatist; simply someone who is self adjusting vs. someone who lives in perpetual internal chaos and confusion! And their outer world usually shows it too!

Renewal of the Mind

Conquering or mastering the mind can be called renewing the mind, which is why Paul wrote to the Romans saying,

> *Do not conform any longer to the pattern of this world, but be transformed by the renewing of your mind. Then you will be able to test and approve what God's will is - his good, pleasing and perfect will.*
>
> *(Romans 12:2 NIV)*

Our mind must be renewed. God's salvation includes the mind. The late Dr Bob Gordon said, "The mind is an actual battlefield in the experience of many people. Lack of mental discipline leads to chaos in the thought life, an inability to discern truth from error and bondage to an imagination that is able to breed negative ideas and dreams."

In her bestseller, *"The Battlefield of the Mind"* Joyce Meyer also states that there is a war going on where our minds are the battlefield, the good news being that God is fighting on our side! Joyce uncovers the tactics of the enemy and gives a clear-cut plan to triumph in the fight for your mind.

She teaches how to renew the mind through the Word and stand victoriously in the battlefield of the mind. Our enemy uses a deliberately devised plan of deceit and lies. His plan is to attack our minds with doubting thoughts, fear and paranoia so that our resistance levels are eroded *(like the immune system)*. He will invest any amount of time it takes to bring defeat in our lives to steal, kill and destroy.

However the Word of God has the power to cleanse our minds regardless and it is all-important that we read and meditate on His Word and remaining obedient to it. We must read, meditate and speak the Word continually, taking captive every thought to make it obedient to Christ (2 Corinthians 10:5). *"Do not let this book of the law depart from your mouth; meditate on it day and night, so that you may be careful to do everything written in it. Then you will be prosperous and successful"* (Joshua 1:8 NIV).

The weaknesses of the natural mind:

- It is hostile to God *(Romans 8:5-7)* unbelievers are often "hostile" towards the gospel
- The things of God are foolish to the natural mind *(1 Corinthians 2:12-14)*
- The natural mind is blinded to God by Satan *(2 Corinthians 4:4)*
- The natural mind is the source of violent and evil desires *(Ephesians 2:3)*
- The natural mind is futile in its thinking and darkened in its understanding *(Ephesians 4:17-18)*

Perhaps you can imagine how Joshua might have felt after he had just successfully crossed over the Jordan River through an awesome act of faith; which took him and all the people across only to arrive at Jericho to look up and see "those gigantic walls" that surrounded that great city.

As a military man his mind must have gone to work strategizing, *"Well if we build some ramps, we'll come at it like this... we can make a hole and maybe get through..."* But instead of *"attacking"* the walls, God's instructions were to "march" around it in silence for seven long and probably hot days - surely this sounded so foolish to Joshua's naturally military mind!

Joshua was as natural as you or I and it would have been as much of a discipline for him as it is for us, to learn to stop thinking in his natural mind, and be disciplined enough to flow with the mind of God, especially when the instructions seemed so completely "un-natural" and out of sync with his natural instincts! And as a military figure Joshua had to lay his own strategy down in order to accept the Lord's.

This is not always easy. But then submission rarely is! It's based on trust, faith and relationship AND dying to self! But as we know on the seventh day when they all marched around in obedience seven times "shouting and praising" the Lord, it was then and only then - out of sheer obedience and discipline - that the walls came tumbling down. Let's be honest, it takes a disciplined mind just to keep our mouths quiet! *"For out of the abundance (overflow) of the heart, his mouth speaks!" (Luke 6:45 AMP)*

Finally remember this - faith is not chatty or spontaneous - it is too deliberate! And disciplining our minds has to be a determined - on purpose - and deliberate act of our faith. Only this will get the job done, no matter how long it takes. Then and only then can we truly say that we have conquered our own minds and now have *"the mind of Christ" (1 Corinthians 2:16).*

❖

CHAPTER 8

Signs of a Renewed Mind

Be Well Informed

Casting down imaginations, and every high thing that exalteth itself against the knowledge of God, and bringing into captivity every thought to the obedience of Christ... (2 Corinthians 10:4-5)

First I want to give you some examples from scripture of what a *"renewed mind"* looks like!

- Our spiritual understanding is increased *(Ephesians 1:18)*

- Our minds become the vehicle of the Holy Spirit and His gifts, discernment and revelation

- We have a changed life through understanding truth

  We must take the cleansing power of God's Word to sanctify our minds and set us free from wrong thoughts. Paul in Ephesians told us to put off the old self which is being corrupted by its deceitful desires, to be made new in the attitude of our minds; and to put on the "new" self, created to be like God in true righteousness and holiness *(see Ephesians 4:22-24; Hebrews 4:12)*

- We have surrendered our minds completely as well as our bodies to the Lord *(Romans 12:1)*

Wrestling with God

I remember Ian Andrews once saying, that when he began to minister in the early 70's, he was told to *"go and preach the gospel"* but by the time he had stuttered out the words *"g o o d - m o r n i n g"* it was already *afternoon!* Ian prayed *"Lord heal me of my stutter and 'then' I will go and preach the gospel for You."*

Nonetheless people were still going to Ian with all kinds of stuttering problems and were getting healed *left-right-and-centre*, which made it even more frustrating for him. However through that process, God taught Ian Andrews how to rely totally on the Holy Spirit and not upon his own understanding, strengths, circumstances or facts *(a good lesson for all of us!)*

Yet Ian had suffered with a *severe* stammer for most of his life and would say to God, *"Lord I'd be thrilled to preach the gospel and pray for the sick - only heal me first."*

But God had the last word on the subject and would say to him, *"No! You go as you are, then everyone will know who the Healer is, that it is Me - I will heal you gradually - AS YOU GO"* and that is precisely what happened! God did it! "AS HE WENT - IN OBEDIENCE!"

For Ian, it was a humbling and sometimes frustrating experience and yet he found that yielding to God was the only way forwards. And to his surprise, God's life began to flow through him as people got healed and most importantly it did not ever depend on Ian or how he felt. Pure and simple - when the people heard that Jesus took their pains and sicknesses upon Himself, they looked to God and were healed.

His Divine Help

Our greatest need right now as Christians is the Holy Spirit - He is the only one who can help us understand the profoundness of all of these things. He alone can show us just how to go about renewing our minds. These few steps are part of the process:

First we must completely surrender our minds to the Lord *(Romans 12:1)*. Complete means complete! This is not a weight watchers plan that we join for a few weeks till normal life takes over - NO! This is God we are talking about - and what He does in our lives is for KEEPS. The idea is this, we give Him our minds and He gives us the Mind of Christ. It's more than a fair deal I would say!!! In fact it is a pure act of grace.

- We must submit all of our *"thinking"* to the cross *(2 Corinthians 10:5)*

- We must make continual and deliberate choices about where we place of our minds *(Colossians 3:2)*

- We must always read and meditate on the cleansing power of God's Word *(Joshua 1:8)*

- Examine and test the content of our thought lives, whatever tries to ENTER we must test. Is this of God, the flesh or Satan? Is this carnal or godly? *(Philippians 4:6-7)*

- We must immediately refuse every thought that is wrong or sinful. God's Word says that we should think of things that are honest and true, the devil says we should think of things that are dishonest and untrue *(Philippians 4:8-9)*

Think God's Thoughts

We must not calculate with human reasoning. For instance when Jesus explained to His disciples how He must go to Jerusalem to suffer many things *(even unto death)*, Peter actually *scolded* Him by saying; *"Never, Lord! This shall never happen to you!"*

Jesus reaction was to turn to him and say, *"'Get behind Me, Satan!' You are a stumbling block to me; you do **not have in mind the things of God,** but the things of men" (Matthew 16:21-23 NIV). Consider this... just momentarily. Ponder on what He said, "...you have not IN MIND the things of God but the things of men."*

70

Now this is not hard to understand, it's not rocket science! What we have in MIND is absolutely everything. Therefore for the serious Christian we better mind the things of God and not the things of this world.

It is not enough to think about something that needs our decision or prayer. We must think about it the way God thinks about it. God's thoughts went beyond the suffering that Jesus would encounter in Jerusalem, beyond the rejection, humiliation, the cross and the grave. In fact God's thoughts looked forward to the resurrection; the triumphant Ascension, the outpouring of the Holy Spirit, to Christ's glorious Second Coming, and ultimately towards His reign upon this earth.

Meditate on the Word

Do not let this book of the law depart from your mouth; meditate on it day and night... successful.
(Joshua 1:8 NIV)

Finally, brothers, whatever is true, whatever is noble, whatever is right, whatever is pure, whatever is lovely, whatever is admirable - if anything is excellent or praiseworthy - think about such things. Whatever you have learned or received or heard from me, or seen in me - put it into practice. And the God of peace will be with you.
(Philippians 4:8-9 NIV)

We must secure all pertinent information concerning our goals. *"Wise men lay up knowledge..."* (Proverbs 10:14 AMP) *"My people are destroyed for lack of knowledge..."* (Hosea 4:6 AMP)

Observe. Read. Maintain an "information file." Utilise the expertise of others. *"He that walketh with wise men shall be wise..." (Proverbs 13:20)*

Create a Climate of Confidence

We must speak about our EXPECTATIONS of SUCCESS, not our EXPERIENCES or FAILURES. *"Death and life are in the power of the tongue..." (Proverbs 18:21 AMP)* We must rehearse previous achievements in our minds and remember that our *"sufficiency is of God..." "In whom we have BOLDNESS and access with CONFIDENCE by the faith of him" (2 Corinthians 3:5; Ephesians 3:11).*

Our position of superiority over circumstances was established when we became children of God *(Romans 8:16, 17, 37).*

Assist others in discovering their gifts, talents and dreams. You will reap what you sow. The motto of the WAY OF THE WINNER is, *"What you make happen for others, God will make happen to you."* When Job prayed for his friends, his captivity was turned *(Job 42:10).* When the poor widow gave to the prophet, God gave to her *(1 Kings 17). "Knowing that whatsoever good thing any man doeth, the same shall he receive of the Lord" (Ephesians 6:8).*

Recognise God as a plus factor. He is NEVER a DIS-ADVANTAGE to us, ALWAYS an ASSET. He wants us to succeed and He has "pleasure in the prosperity of His servant" *(Psalm 35:27).* Read scriptures on a daily schedule. Practice the power of prayer.

Make Jesus Christ Lord of your life. *"Acquaint now thyself with him, and be at peace: thereby good shall come unto thee"* (Job 22:21) *"...as long as he sought the Lord, God made him to prosper"* (2 Chronicles 26:5).

Finally we can say that Life only changes when our daily priorities change.

❖

CHAPTER 9

Don't Speak Until God gives the Key!

Life and Death are in the Tongue

My wife recently reminded me of a story that a pastor once told us when in Entebbe, Uganda together quite some years ago now. He told the congregation and us about an experience he had with some dogs!

Wherefore, holy brethren, partakers of the heavenly calling, consider the Apostle and High Priest of our profession, Christ Jesus.

(Hebrews 3:1)

However I must interject here, that dogs in Africa are not held in the same regard as they are in much of Europe and other countries. For instance they are not considered "domestic" animals but much like yard dogs, guard dogs or even hunting dogs – but certainly never kept indoors with the family – only ever outside! *(This is not to mention such places as I have travelled, where eating dog-meat is common – but that's a whole other story!)*

Anyhow, this pastor continued to tell of the time when he owned a kennel full of dogs. On having heard about the power of words from the bible for the first time, he embarked on putting such a theory to the test! He chose just two dogs for his experiment then proceeded by putting them in separate cages and for a period of several weeks spoke life to one and death to the other.

During the experiment he kept up a daily routine; each time he fed the dogs, he would hurl abuse at one, but blessing and encouragement to the other! However the experiment got outside of his control.

He witnessed with his own eyes how, after just some weeks into his experiment, that the dog with which he had spoke words of death, had slowly began to die. Once he noticed this for certain, *(after an approximate six week period)* and feeling sad for the dog, he attempted to reverse the experiment by speaking the same words of live that he had spoken to the other dog – which was incidentally thriving and healthy!

However it became evident, that it was too late to turn things around and that death had indeed taken hold of that poor dog which sadly died. A strong lesson not easily forgotten and something that my wife has never forgotten either!

What a crude and cruel experiment? Yes! But in his youthful ignorance, this pastor found out, in his rather rudimentary way, the exact extent of his words. Evidence that words have great power for - life or death – no matter who we are and no matter where we come from.

Self-inflicted Wounds

Dr Mike Murdock in his book, *"Wisdom for Winning"* wrote about a friend who "…noted an inner depression when he indulged in revealing the flaws of others." For this we can turn to Proverbs 18:8 in the Young's Literal Translation of the bible, where it says very clearly:

*The words of a talebearer are as **self-inflicted wounds**, and they have gone down to the inner parts of the heart.*
(Proverbs 18:8 YLT)

The mouthpiece becomes the victim! The pastor, who watched his own dog slowly dying as a direct result of his words, deeply regretted his experiment and his initial doubt in God's Word.

Gladly when we do believe God He can bring about total healing through His Word:

Whoso keepeth his mouth and his tongue keepeth his soul from troubles.
(Proverbs 21:23)

Faith filled Words

Jesus can only use our faith filled words to fulfil His purposes. Any other words we speak will be judged. Matthew 12:36 says that we will be judged for every idle *(or careless)* word that we speak.

In fact the International Standard Bible Encyclopedia (ISBE) states that the Greek word *(argós)* generally used for *"idle or idleness"* in the New Testament literally meant, *inactive, useless, empty gossip, nonsensical talk.* Whereas the *Strong's Concordance #G692* takes *argos (pronounced ar-gos')* as generally meaning; *inactive, unemployed; lazy, useless; barren, idle or slow.*

So this means that Jesus will either use or only judge our words. With this in mind James warns that if our tongue is unbridled it can actually *"...set on fire the course of our life, and is set on fire by hell"* *(James 3:6 NASB).*

In Hebrews 3:1 however we are instructed to; *"Consider the Apostle and High Priest of our profession, Christ [or the Anointed One] Jesus"* and the word translated as *"profession"* in that verse can also be translated as *"confession."* This means that God appointed Jesus to be our High Priest, only over our confession - which is our *"declaration of FAITH."*

Having said all this; both our words - faith filled words and our words of idleness have affected our lives up to this point. In fact we could say that our lives today are the *"direct-result"* of our own consistent choice of words. So perhaps now's the time to change our vocabulary, especially those who don't like themselves very much!

True to His Word, Jesus Christ as the Apostle and High Priest will faithfully back our words - but only when we speak what God says in His Word. Think about it, God placed such a high premium on "words" purely because He can only "agree" with His own Word in our mouths, and this is what He wants to bring to pass. It is a total revelation to some that mere "words" can be so literally powerful that they can change the very course of our eternal destiny.

As Christian's we have an out-and-out obligation to speak "right words" and what a difference they can make! We all know that from the very beginning of our experience with Christ, we came head to head with the power of words and the awesome difference that they can make, "...*if thou shalt confess with thy mouth the Lord Jesus, and shalt believe in thine heart that God hath raised him from the dead, thou shalt be saved" (Romans 10:9)*.

Words Mingled with Truth

Many people around the world confess faith in Jesus as their Lord and Saviour and proclaim that God had raised Him from the dead, as a result are no longer hell bound, but heaven bound! Mere words mingled with truth and faith changed their eternal destiny forever. But we must also consider that if words can change destiny, words can also change anything!

There is power in words. In fact the spiritual forces of life or death are released through our words alone. This means that beyond our conversion experience we must continue to make the right choices with our words! Knowing God's Word is essential for this. And by speaking right words like this we can help steer the course that God wants us to take; knowing every word we speak will affect everyone else around us; for good or for bad.

What an awesome responsibility we have. All the idle and fruitless chatter we once enjoyed is now a privilege we can no longer indulge ourselves in. For when we committed ourselves to Christ we also committed our mouths to Him. This we can never change; our mouths are too significant to trifle with; either they are fountains of life or death, blessing or cursing, something becomes too serious to be jovial about, especially as one matures in Christ. We are totally accountable.

He's Committed to Faith

Once again Jesus is not committed to any words that we speak; only to spoken-words of faith that agree with His and as High Priest of our confession *(spoken faith in His Word)*, Jesus becomes obligated to **bring-those-words-to-PASS,** but let me point out that it is the Holy Spirit who **brings-them-to-LIFE.**

We see this in John 6:63 *(AMP)* where it says;

> It is the Spirit Who gives life [He is the Life-giver]; the flesh conveys no benefit whatever [there is no profit in it]. The words (truths) that I have been speaking to you are spirit and life.

Think about it, if the very words that Jesus spoke were inspired and brought to life by the Holy Spirit how much more do we need the help! **So our High Priest and the Holy Spirit work together,** to bring our words to life and to pass!

> *...the word is very near you, in your mouth and in your mind and in your heart, so that you can do it.*
> *(Deuteronomy 30:14 AMP, also Romans 10:8)*

Then 1 Corinthians 1:4-5 also tells us that Jesus enriches our utterance. That is, He takes our words of faith and enriches them with His. So no matter how we look at it, **the words we speak have the ability to carry the very creative force of almighty God behind them.** What weight that is! And they are "bound" to come to pass! *"I thank my God... Jesus Christ; that in everything ye are enriched by him, in all utterance, and in all knowledge..."*

As mentioned before God intended us to be the prophet of our own lives, so that we could bring good things to pass by using our mouths to "affirm" His Word. *"...out of the abundance of the heart the mouth speaketh. A good man out of the good treasure of the heart **bringeth forth** good things..."* *(Matthew 12:34-37)*

It's evident therefore that an opportunity exists to all of us; to **bring forth** life or to **bring forth** death. Some people imagine that their words don't *"bring forth"* anything! But for those of us who understand differently and have had this "revealed" to us by the Holy Spirit, now have a responsibility to act upon what we know.

For the rest of our lives we must act wisely - every single time we open our mouths! No longer can we leisurely engage in idle chatter. On the other hand we can still be spontaneous and free - sure! - But with restraint and self-control, knowing that EVERY word will be judged.

To finish I heard Ulf Ekman once say, **"Put a padlock on your mouth and only speak when God gives you the key!"**

❖

CHAPTER 10

The Perils of Disappointment

Tactics of our Adversary

It's easy in this life to become disappointed; in fact who hasn't been at some point or another? Ministry in particular is an arena where disappointment can thrive! As a minister I had to learn a long time ago not to allow disappointment to get me down. It is all too easy to give into the feelings of disappointment, mainly where other people are involved *(especially when other ministers let you down!)*

They trusted you and were never disappointed.
(Psalm 22:5 GW)

By measure of necessity, I learnt to get over disappointment as quickly as possible; the alternative is for un-forgiveness to set in which only taints our inner focus *(spiritual sight)* rendering us un-available to be used by God any longer.

Disappointment is *a firm for-runner for un-forgiveness* and a sure tactic of our adversary who desires to get us over into disappointment for as long as possible so that un-forgiveness sets in. This of course traps us until we repent, but our enemy knows that many Christians have become so dull spiritually that they are totally unaware they are even walking in un-forgiveness.

Our opponent has watched the human-experience from the beginning of time and knows just where to blind-side us, especially using the realm of our emotions. At all costs we must keep our emotions in check - because this arena alone gives Satan all the opportunity he needs. If given an inch, he always takes a mile; we must not give him that opportunity.

There are many words that describe disappointments character perfectly. In fact most words have at least one synonym *(descriptive word with identical meaning)*. The following are synonyms of disappointment: *dissatisfaction, displeasure, distress, discontent, disenchantment, dis-illusionment, frustration and regret.*

Common to all Men

Anyone who has ever stepped into disappointment, even if just for a single day, will be familiar with these as well. In fact I doubt there is a person alive who hasn't experienced all of them! 1 Corinthians 10:13 teaches us that there is no temptation that is not common to all men, making it safe to assume that anyone and everyone has tasted this bitter-pill called disappointment at some point or another!

We are all tempted to get into it because it's just like any other seductive temptation; we are lured into disappointment through emotions - but we must avoid this at any expense because it only leads to bitterness which in turn leads to un-forgiveness which in-avertedly costs us everything.

From a personal front, some years ago my wife was deeply affected by disappointment. I have said before, ministry is a breeding ground for this because some of the things that people are prepared to say or do at times - can be nothing short of treachery! Scripture is clear about treachery, in fact Isaiah said, "Traitors continue to betray, and their *treachery* grows worse and worse" *(Isaiah 24:16 GW)* and in Psalm 78:57 it says, "They were disloyal and *treacherous...* like arrows shot from a defective bow!" *(GW)*

Over a prolonged period of time, my wife had watched the behaviour of certain respectable people who lacked certain discretions and as a result became increasingly disillusioned with all-things-ministry simply through this type of deep-seated disappointment that had lodged in her heart.

Harmless enough one might presume, but it did some damage, however thankfully she recovered; but there are many who don't. Actually there are many today who have left the ministry for this same reason and never returned. We are talking about reality here! None of us should give ourselves over to anything - because what starts with mere emotion ends up more critical - if left to germinate!

When all Seems Lost

David knew this well and he had reason to be distressed at times especially in 1 Samuel chapter 30:1-6 when after returning home, he discovered that his own people were about to kill him. In addition everything he owned was either burnt to the ground or taken captive *(kidnapped!)* "David and his men came to the city, and, behold, *it was* burned with fire; and their wives, and their sons, and their daughters, were taken captives.

Then David and the people that *were* with him lifted up their voice and wept, until they had no more power to weep..." *(30:3-4 NIV)* In verse 6 we see David clearly distressed by the situation but instead of nervously reacting to the crisis we see him responding to it by faith;

> **David was greatly distressed;** *for the people spoke of stoning him, because the soul of all the people was grieved, every man for his sons and for his daughters:* **but David encouraged himself in the LORD his God.**
> *(1 Samuel 30:6 NIV)*

Almost deranged with grief, David's own people had risen up against him with a united front, wanting to exact-punishment for their joint loss. In other words they wanted someone to blame and take their grief out on. *(Note: the first rule of leadership "everything is your fault!")*

Now it's understandable that they did not want to party at this point, and they were themselves disappointed in David, perhaps they thought that his leadership or mismanagement cost them everything? However many of us at times have felt like the whole world was against us which brought us great personal "distress."

Inner Defence Mechanism

This is when we need to employ the same secret weapon that David had. An *"inner-defence-mechanism"* that would not allow the disappointments and stresses of life to overcome him. As over-comers, we too must learn to encourage ourselves in the Lord, to offset the disappointments in our own lives *(Revelation 2:7, 11, 26; 3:5, 12, 21)*.

If the anointed kings of the bible had to keep themselves encouraged we are certainly not immune to the stresses of life, even with Christ on our side! It takes discipline and David would have developed this into his life, long before he ever went to battle.

Resisting disappointment is as much an act-of-the-will as is patience. These healthy responses to life sadly don't come to us naturally *(automatically)* instead we must work at them voluntarily until they become part of our natural responses to life. *(Remember our flesh is like a rebellious dog that must be tamed. Needing strong discipline until it's not necessary anymore!)*

Fundamentally and relationally disappointment means to fail to satisfy an expectation. Disappointment will always be on this earth, and as mentioned above, the most important thing is not what happens but how we respond to it! If allowed to affect us, disappointment has the ability to destroy our faith.

It can make us angry with God, at others and at ourselves and can be all consuming. I have met folks who are just so very angry all the time. The sad fact is that they experienced just one too many disappointments in their life - never overcame it - and as a result live angry with themselves and with the world *(everyone in it)* for the rest of their lives!

However this type of anger, which comes from disappointment, can consume our faith. I have seen people get so turned on to the Word of God and then when things don't work out as they had planned; disappointment sets in and their faith rapidly disappears. People can literally float on cloud nine for weeks until a *"suddenly"* occurs and then the disappointment bomb drops and their bubble bursts forever!

Perceived Injury

Disappointment can also cause many people to backslide. I have seen more people backslide through disappointment than anything else. People get disappointed in each other, and even turn their back on the Lord Jesus Christ because of it. But regardless of what anyone else does, the Word of God does not change and nor should we.

Then there are the unfounded or imagined disappointments; which are the same thing as perceived-injury, something that I have taught on quite abundantly over the years because many people suffer from this; especially common in the Body of Christ! Vain imaginations are the culprit, which make us perceive that people are doing an injury when they actual are not.

Life is just one big mind game, one that we *must* win; we are over-comers in Christ. To achieve this we must first know His Word and not be willing to deviate from it, to the left hand or the right, because it's the only sure foundation we have. It offers us pure-security when the rest of the world is swimming with disappointment, fear and insecurity.

Finally in Proverbs 31:27 it talks about the bread of discontent and self-pity!

> *She looks well to how things go in her household, and the bread of idleness (gossip, discontent, and self-pity) she will not eat.*
>
> (Proverbs 31:27 AMP)

Discontentment means; unhappiness, irritation, annoyance, disapproval and anger. Disillusionment is similar in meaning to disappointment but also means; lack of expectation, cynicism and disenchantment.

We must guard against these opponents of our faith.

❖

CHAPTER 11

Double Mindedness
Doubt & Unbelief

The Two Spirited Man

Let us first look at double mindedness; which is designed to stop us receiving from God and in fact is synonymous with being double-spirited. If you look up this word *"double-minded"* in the Authorized Version of the bible (KJV) and use the Strong's Concordance or the Vines dictionary to discover its original Greek meaning you will find that double-minded *(δίψυχος dipsychos)* actually means **"two-spirited!"**

A person who has doubts shouldn't expect to receive anything from the Lord... A person who has doubts is thinking about two different things at the same time and can't make up his mind about anything.

(James 1:6-8 GW)

Now this adds a whole new emphasis on being double minded! In other words we cannot successfully live in two different kingdoms or operate in two different spirits at the same time, *(i.e. the spirit of this world and the spirit of God - the kingdom of God and the kingdom of darkness)* it just does not function *(see Strong's #G1374).*

In fact being double minded and doubting is practically the same thing, so when we step into doubt, we step into instability as verse 8 tells that a double minded person is "...unstable in all of his ways." Doubt literally means *to waver in judgement; to hesitate in indecision and to distrust.* Most Christians find themselves - at some point - in this sad condition and then wonder why they are **spiritually and emotionally confused!**

Contingency Arrangement

For example, when asked, most Christians would say that they believe what the Word says about a situation but also admit that they always have a *"Plan B" (contingency arrangement!)* just in case it doesn't quite work out as God said it would! **That's like going forwards only to go backwards!** James 1:5-8 says;

*...let him ask in faith, nothing wavering. For he that wavereth is like a wave of the sea driven with the wind and tossed. For **let not that man think that he shall receive anything of the Lord.***

Now unbelief is different to double mindedness or doubt in that it won't even "consider" Plan A; instead it just "deserts" God altogether as seen here in Hebrews 3:12 (AMP);

...brethren, take care, lest there be in any one of you a wicked, unbelieving heart [which refuses to cleave to, trust in, and rely on Him], **leading you to turn away and desert...the living God.**

This scripture clearly warns against the unbelieving heart that "refuses to... trust." In fact from the very onset unbelief is decidedly **negative, unreasonable and faithless;** where doubters are a little more subtle in their contemplation; *"I believe God's Word; it's just not working for me!"* Unbelief on the other hand, has no intention of flowing with God.

In fact, unbelief cannot be accused of being double-minded at all; with its flat refusal to believe! It is simply hostile to God; again Hebrews above warns of the wicked-ness of the unbelieving heart but here in Romans 8:6 it talks of the sheer hostility of the carnal mind towards God.

Now the mind of the flesh [which is sense and reason without the Holy Spirit] is death *[death that comprises all the miseries arising from sin, both here and hereafter].*

But the mind of the [Holy] Spirit is life and [soul] peace [both now and forever]. [That is] because **the mind of the flesh [with its carnal thoughts and purposes] is hostile to God, for it does not submit itself to God's Law; indeed it cannot.**

(Romans 8:6 AMP)

In other words doubt wavers between making decisions, where unbelief has already decided! "How long halt ye between two opinions? If the LORD be God, follow him: but if Baal, then follow him. And the people answered him not a word" *(1 Kings 18:21).*

A Satanic Force

So there you have it, pure and simple; unbelief is a satanic force and is unambiguous *(clear-cut)* in its approach. It holds itself to a complete-denial of deity and refusal of truth. For instance there is always someone who will say, *"I believe that speaking in tongues is of the devil."* This in itself is refusing God's Word not doubting it.

There are many people in unbelief today simply because they do not believe the verity of God's Word. We even have theologians who teach that angels do not exist while in the New Testament Jesus Himself told of how the angels came to feed and minister to Him. In the Old Testament for instance - Psalm 91 - it is unquestionably talking about angels! So although clearly present in His Word they still deny it!

Then there are those who say there is no devil. Well then I can only say that Jesus must have been **hallucinating** or imagined some weird and wonderful happenings out there in the desert! However the Word clearly says that the devil tempted Jesus in the wilderness; in fact Jesus Himself told us that we would cast out devils in His name *(Mark 16:17-18).*

It is sad to say that those who consider themselves to be *"believers"* are the ones who often suffer from unbelief the most! In fact in Africa *(where I have travelled extensively)*, Europe is known as the **"dark continent"** which has churches full of **"unbelieving believers!"**

What a parody *(distortion)* and a poor legacy that we have left the rest of the world! In fact it's a spiritual travesty!

❖

CHAPTER 12

The Perils of Fear

The Spirit of Dread

In the previous chapter we looked at the subjects of **double-mindedness, doubt and unbelief** but now we must look at the participation that **fear** plays. As revealed in the following scripture, fear and unbelief work very closely together, if not hand in hand!

*He that overcometh shall inherit all things; and I will be his God, and he shall be my son. But the **fearful, and unbelieving,** and the abominable, and murderers, and whoremongers, and sorcerers, and idolaters, and all liars, **shall have their part in the lake, which burneth with fire and brimstone:** which is the second death.*

(Revelation 21:7-9)

In actual fact it's also worth noting that the "fearful and unbelieving" take pole position above "murderers" on the list of who will end up in the lake of fire. Quite shocking! However we must be determined to view the spirit of fear and unbelief in the same way that God does. So let's look more closely what the Word says about it, particularly fear.

As mentioned in the scripture above the word used for *"fear"* in the original Greek *(δειλός deilos)* comes from a root word *deos* meaning to *"dread"* or to be *"timid"* and implies *"unfaithfulness" (see Strong's #G1169).*

Interestingly the word used for *"unbelieving"* - in the original Greek *(compound word)* primarily means; *"faithless, passive and untrustworthy." (Also see: ap'-is-tos #G571 and #G4103. This is also a compound word where we see that "pistos" [belief] becomes "a-pistos." The addition of an "a-" in front of pistos [belief] brings it into the negative form - just as adding "un-" to belief makes it un-belief!)*

Now there are those who reckon that there is such a thing in the bible as *"the-law-of-first-mention."* This is debatable of course, but if we were to take this literally, that would make the positioning of *"fear" (principal)* and *"unbelief" (successive).* This list of doom in Revelations reveals much to us, considering the entire list such as the "abominable *(repulsive and detestable)* and murderers, idolaters and liars..."

Fear and unbelief come out "top" of a very nasty list, which reveals just how offensive they must be to God. Other translations prefer to use the words like *"cowardly and unfaithful"* instead of *"fearful and unbelieving."* **Nevertheless,** revealed major offences to God like this need to get our attention.

Incompetent Spineless and Disloyal

The Amplified uses words like: *"cowards... ignoble... contemptible ...cravenly lacking in courage... cowardly submissive... unbelieving and faithless."* Whereas the Message Bible simply calls such people, *"feckless and faithless"* which means: **"incompetent, spineless and disloyal!"**

Evidently we must make sure that we are not preaching a false gospel, one that is politically correct yet utterly powerless to produce strength in the lives of its people. Producing instead converts who think that it's okay to be incompetent, spineless and disloyal. Such people will wake up to a rude shock one day, along with their teachers, who will be held accountable for propagating such *weaknesses.*

*Not many [of you] should become teachers (self-constituted censors and reprovers of others), my brethren, for you know that we [teachers] will be judged by a higher standard and with greater severity [than other people; thus **we assume the greater accountability and the more condemnation**].*

(James 3:1 AMP)

*Don't be in any rush to become a teacher, my friends. **Teaching is highly responsible work. Teachers are held to the strictest standards.***

(James 3:1 MSG)

Thankfully, as true Disciples of Christ, we are not spineless and faint-hearted! For we are no longer enslaved to the spirit of fear that is in this world. Instead we have been empowered through Christ, to live for Him without fear, dread or any kind of shame. In God we are powerful not pitiful. He does not want us to grovel and crawl around before Him in cowering, squirming docility.

This scripture below paints an entirely different picture. Through God's Spirit in us, we are stable and formidable not slimy and pathetic!

God did not give us a spirit of timidity (of cowardice, of craven and cringing and fawning fear), but [He has given us a spirit] of power and of love and of calm and well-balanced mind and discipline and self-control. Do not blush or be ashamed then, to testify to and for our Lord... take your share of the suffering [to which the preaching] of the Gospel [may expose you, and do it] in the power of God.

(2 Timothy 1:6-8 AMP)

The condition is that we trust and love God above all else: *"I will say of the Lord, He is my Refuge and my Fortress, my God;* **on Him I lean and rely, and in Him I [confidently] trust... Because he has set his love upon Me, therefore will I deliver him..."** *(Psalm 91:2, 14 AMP)* *"All things work together and are [fitting into a plan] for good to and* **for those who love God** *and are called according to [His] design and purpose"* *(Romans 8:28 AMP).*

In addition Isaiah declared from the Old Testament:

> *Fear not [there is nothing to fear], for I am with you;* *do not look around you in terror and be dismayed, for I am your God. I will strengthen and harden you to difficulties,* *yes, I will help you; yes, I will hold you up and retain you with My [victorious] right hand of rightness and justice.*
>
> *(Isaiah 41:10 AMP)*

Fear is Faith in Reverse Gear

> *Now faith is the assurance (the confirmation, the title deed) of the things [we] hope for, being the proof of things [we] do not see and the conviction of their reality [faith perceiving as real fact what is not revealed to the senses].*
>
> *(Hebrews 11:1 AMP)*

To look more closely at the characteristics of fear, it could be said that fear behaves much like faith, but in reverse gear! Think about that for a moment. If faith is the *"substance"* or *"assurance"* of good things desired, fear is also the *"substance"* or *"assurance"* of bad things NOT desired.

If we look in the Message Bible again, at Hebrews 11:1, it reads like this: "This faith… it's our handle on what we can't see." I like that! **Because it's important for us to recognise that fear also sees. But it only sees things in the NEGATIVE.** *(Someone who is usually negative or sour all the time, usually suffers from or is in bondage to a tormenting spirit of fear in his or her mind).*

To move on I want to yet again turn to the Greek (#G5287 *in the Strong's*) where we can discover that *"substance"* or *"assurance"* that is used in Hebrews 11:1 also means, *"concrete essence."* This would allow verse 1 to be read something like this; *"Faith brings the 'concrete essence' of things expected and the proof of things not yet seen."*

Reverse this equation and it could read like this instead: *"fear (acting as faith in reverse) brings the 'concrete essence' of those negative things expected and the proof of negative things not yet seen!"* This is confirmed by what Jesus told the centurion, *"...go thy way; and as thou hast believed, so be it done unto thee"* (*Matthew 8:13*).

However if we go to verse 3 of the Message Bible it reads: *"By faith, we see the world called into existence by God's word, what we see created by what we don't see."* This is so profoundly simple but I want us to get this.

It helps to paraphrase this: *"By fear, we see negative things called into existence by our words, what we see created by what we don't see."* It is within Satan's interest to continually feed us with fear orientating thoughts, with the hope that our faith becomes dis-orientated (*mixed-up, confused, dazed!*)

When someone is orientating us, they are by definition: positioning, angling, facing and even familiarizing us with something. Think about this! If Satan can get us more accustomed to thinking in terms of fear than faith; if he can familiarize us more with the negative – then he can achieve incubation.

102

He knows that, *"what you feed, you breed!"* That's why every media possible is touting his message. Continually feeding society and brain washing them, conditioning them to the point where they really begin to believe the deception.

It is within human nature for us to start talking about what we believe. If it's in our hearts, our mouths will begin to leak. It's hard to supress! We just need to ensure that what we believe is the right things, as it is written:

> *I believed; therefore I have spoken. With that same spirit of faith we also believe and therefore speak...*
> *(2 Corinthians 4:13 NIV)*

History proves that people throughout the ages, have been able to adapt themselves to whatever they have been continually familiarized with.

Therefore it's an absolute necessity for us as believers to watch what we are feeding on, just like Joshua was warmed in chapter 1:8 to, *"meditate... night and day"* (*which notably leaves time for little else!*) However it's undeniable, regardless of culture, time or race – but whatever is going IN will eventually come OUT. We know that, *"faith comes from hearing (and feeding on)... the word of Christ"* (*Romans 10:17 NIV*).

Once again, it is our clearheaded duty to watch what we are focussing on, on a daily basis. Our mental focus will eventually become our verbal focus as well. We must fill our minds and therefore our mouths NOT with the negative (*that which is nurtured by fear*) but with faith (*that which is nourished by the very Word of God).* **"Nourished up in the words of faith and of good doctrine..."** *(1 Timothy 4:6)*

Faith is Not an Emotion

Admittedly there are times when believing is the last thing we feel like doing especially in a crisis, but that's when we must understand that **faith is not an emotion it is a decision!** In fact, generally speaking if we wait for our emotions to motivate us - we would never do anything significant for God *(when emotions fail, faith remains robust).*

In fact fear is actually putting our faith in what the devil can do rather than what God can do. Having said this, fear and faith are not on equal-par *(faith is far greater)* and perhaps this is why fear is so offensive to God. However the chief reason that any of us fear something is because we are really convinced that it will come to pass. That's what worry is all about. If we didn't believe it could come to pass - then there would be no reason to worry!

Worry in itself is counter-productive and energy zapping, because it cannot stop anything, it is passive and can only dwell on the negatives *(or the problem)* instead of the solution which **only helps *"draw"* the trouble closer!** Job is the classic example of this truth.

> *For the thing which I greatly fear comes upon me, and that of which I am afraid befalls me. I was not or am not at ease, nor had I or have I rest, nor was I or am I quiet, yet trouble came and still comes [upon me].*
> *(Job 3:25-26 AMP)*

Job *"practiced"* his fear continually and as a result - his fear was great in strength. Although by way of conflict the scriptures declare that Job dwelt in safety, we see this in the accusation Satan brought against God, *"You've hedged him about on every side, and I can't get to him" (Job 1:6-12).*

Satan's sly request was then for God to *"strike"* everything that Job had, in order to disprove his faith. Now I personally believe that God did not just grant this request out-right but actually replied with a statement of fact instead. See in verse 12 how God said to Satan; *"He **IS** in your power" (AMP).*

In other words, *"he is ALREADY in your power!"* It is important therefore to realize here that God did NOT put Job in that position rather Job put himself there. He found himself in Satan's grasp simply because of the continual ***"fear-rituals"*** he engaged in for his children *(see Job 1:5).* This very fear contributed to the dissembling of his protective hedge and all that he had *(verse 10).* **Remember if we lose our position *(of faith)* we always lose our possession.**

Looking and Listening

Fear therefore gives Satan just the opportunity he is looking for. And yes! He is LOOKING. *"Be sober, be vigilant; because your adversary the devil, as a roaring lion, walketh about, **seeking** whom he may devour..." (1 Peter 5:8-9)* Inevitably fear always puts us in an unfavourable position. Where faith lifts us, fear pulls us down.

This type of fear that takes us where we don't want to go is simply named DREAD and is very effective indeed. When we dread something long enough, we end up doing or saying the exact things we have dreaded and end up in precisely the position we didn't want to be in! Remember Job. His fear came upon him. **Both fear and faith act like magnets - drawing good things or bad towards us. So watch out!**

Dread is forward looking, just like faith, but the negative realm uses our *"imagination"* to help build mind-pictures of those things that we are dreading. This is exactly the same way that faith operates, we must see ourselves - by faith - doing or obtaining the very thing we are reaching for.

The prerequisite *(condition)* is that we must see it before we possess it - naturally. Like the youth who sees themselves driving *"long"* before he or she even goes to driving school! This is faith in operation in simple terms! Or Father Abraham who was required to see himself as the father of many nations before he actually was!

However dread will make us see *(and persistently see)* the very things that we don't want to happen *(dread is synonymous with trepidation, nervousness and anxiety)*. If we yield and think about dreadful things long enough or dwell on them hard enough, then they will eventually be drawn our way! As said previously - this is literally faith in reverse and something we must not engage in.

More importantly it is mounting fear that reverses faith, not just the little fears we all face each day, but the mounting, persisting, tormenting type, that we fail to deal with as we know we should. Job said, *"The thing I've **greatly** feared has come upon me."* Job knew his mistake. He even spelt it out loud and clear!

He was not confused or out of his mind. He knew what brought him down: his own fault. There is no doubt that Job had originally had faith, but he allowed his faith to be swallowed up in fear. Sometimes we have to have faith in our faith - in the context, of what faith can do, *versus* what fear can achieve. It's in our own interest to stand in faith rather than fear. The fringe benefits are much better!

Charles Capps says, ***"When you speak your fears they will grow and nullify your faith. You can't keep the devil from bringing thoughts of doubt and fear to your mind but those things will die unborn if we don't speak them."***

Our words either give our adversary the license and opportunity to move or God - on our behalf. And I know whom I would prefer on my side!

King Solomon understood this when he said, ***"Death and life are in the power of the tongue,*** and they who indulge in it shall eat the fruit of it [for death or life]" *(Proverbs 18:21 AMP).* In the New Testament it says, *"For by your words you will be justified and acquitted, and by your words you will be condemned and sentenced" (Matthew 12:37 AMP).* Ouch what a thought!

Many times however we don't realise the power of our words and the more we speak about negatives the more they grip our heart and multiply in strength. **Fear will establish itself - taking as long as it takes - knowing that if it can establish a strong enough foothold, any individual will eventually lose their strength and ability to deal with it.**

Faith Comes By Hearing

The same way that faith comes by hearing by the Word of God, fear comes by hearing negatives! Our words can create shields of defence or open-opportunities for evil intent.

We build and strengthen our shield *(hedge)* or we weaken it. For example, if we speak fear it insulates us and stops the blessings. You might say a fear filled word produce more fear and invites the enemy to quench the blessings of God *"...he which soweth bountifully shall reap also bountifully"* *(2 Corinthians 9:6)*. It's good to remember that everything can work in its own reverse-state. And bountiful words of spoken-fear can and will reap bountifully - after its own kind.

On the other hand whatever is born of God is victorious over the world; and this is the victory that conquers the world, even our faith *(1 John 5:4 AMP)*. **We can be utterly victorious and unstoppable if we don't yield to fear.**

Faith is stronger than fear and is our victory that overcomes the world and principally comes through faith in God's Word. Heart faith comes from deep within where the Word abides. However we must remember just because we have faith does not automatically mean that we will operate by that faith. Anything can be dormant and passive including our faith.

We must have the faith that we received from God, the very faith of the Son of God *(Galatians 2:20)*.

❖

CONCLUSION

Stop Complaining about the Journey

It always matters what we *LOOK* at… to defeat us or to take us over. Numbers chapter 11 and 21 talk about *"complaining"* and how it angered God, because of this serpents were released into everyone's lives, not *just* those who complained, everyone suffered.

When reading the text, we can see that anxiety and depression affected the children of Israel along their wilderness journey. As a result they began to bitterly complain and speak against God and Moses. They went from victory to pain as many died. This today is considered a mental illness. To keep complaining! This brings misfortune. There is still no blessing in complaining, only *anxiety and depression*.

We don't need psychiatric or psychological help when it is all there in the Word of God – everything we need! "Therefore if any man *be* in Christ, *he is* a new creature: old things are **passed away;** behold, **all things are become new"** *(2 Corinthians 5:17).* This includes behaviour!

If we yield to the Spirit and the fruit of HIS character *(divine nature)* this will totally alter our own behaviour. And when our minds are being renewed daily by the Word, our lives can truly be "transformed."

> *And be not conformed to this world: but be ye <u>transformed</u> by the renewing of your mind, that ye may prove what is that good, and acceptable, and perfect, will of God.*
>   *(Romans 12:2)*

The fruits of the Spirit alter our behaviour, no longer a fallen human behaviour but a surrendered behaviour. The best psychology for mankind is the fruits of the spirit simply because it deals with every human ill and is above the law!

We begin truly to overcome when we can grasp these concepts. **Jesus overcame and gave HIS victory, straight to us.** We are now seated with Him, positioned *above* the problems of life and NOT beneath them; not easily crushed by life. We come from the top down, just like the anointing! "In all these things we are more than conquerors through him that loved us" *(Romans 8:37).*

> *Blessed be the God and Father of our Lord Jesus Christ, who hath blessed us with all spiritual blessings in heavenly places in Christ.*
>   *(Ephesians 1:3)*

And hath raised us up together, and made us sit together in heavenly places in Christ Jesus.

(Ephesians 2:6)

❖

Bibliography

- Andrews, Ian. Equipped to Heal. Copyright © 2010. Published by Onwards and Upwards Publishers. Printed in UK.

- Gordon, Bob. Understanding the Way. Copyright © 1987. Published by Marshall and Scott. Printed in UK.

- Murdock, Mike. Wisdom for Winning. Copyright © 1988. Published by Honor Books. Printed in USA.

- Meyer, Joyce. Battlefield of the Mind. Copyright © 1995. Published by Harrison House, Inc. Printed in USA.

- Orr, James. M.A., D.D., General Editor, International Standard Bible Encyclopedia (ISBE); e-Sword ® version 7.6.1 Copyright © 2000-2005. All Rights Reserved. Registered trade mark of Rick Meyers. Equipping Ministries Foundation. USA www.e-sword.net.

- Strong, James. S.T.D., L.L.D. 1890. Strong's Exhaustive Concordance; Dictionaries of the Hebrew and Greek Words. e-Sword ® version 7.6.1 Copyright © 2000-2005. All Rights Reserved. Registered trade mark of Rick Meyers. Equipping Ministries Foundation. USA www.e-sword.net.

- Unless otherwise indicated, all scriptural quotations are taken from the King James Version of the bible.

❖

Ministry Profile

Doctor Alan Pateman, an apostle, is the President and Founder of **"Alan Pateman Ministries International"** (APMI), which was established in England back in 1987, a Christian-based *(parachurch)* non-profit and non-denominational outreach. This ministry is now focusing in two main areas: First **"Connecting for Excellence"** Apostolic Networking (CFE) and secondly, the teaching arm, **"LifeStyle International Christian University"** (LICU).

CFE is a multi-facetted missions organisation with the purpose of connecting leaders for divine opportunities and building lasting relationships, to touch the lives of leaders literally the world over. Apostle Dr Alan Pateman has to date ordained more than 500 ministers in over 50 NATIONS. In addition there are ministries, churches and schools who are in Association or Affiliation, looking to him for apostolic counsel and oversight.

Secondly LICU, which was founded in 2007, is a study program to help people discover their purpose and destiny. A global network of university campuses and correspondence students, demonstrating the Supernatural Kingdom of God through Doctrinal, Apostolic and Prophetic Teaching. Dr Alan holds the position of President/CEO, Professor of Theology, Biblical Studies and Apostolic Ministry. LICU is exploding throughout Europe, Asia and Africa, enhancing the Body of Christ

Dr Alan has authored more than 35 books including numerous teaching materials and LICU university courses (30) along with hundreds of Truth for the Journey articles on kingdom lifestyle *(that are regularly distributed globally via the internet).*

He is recognised as an Apostle, Bishop, Leadership Mentor, University Educator, Motivational Speaker, Connector and Author, who has also been featured on national and international TV and radio networks throughout the years.

Currently Apostle Alan, his wife Dr Jennifer reside in Lucca *(Tuscany)* Italy and travel out from their Apostolic Company.

- Alan Pateman Ph.D., D.Min., D.D., M.A., B.Th.

Academic Background

Dr. Alan Pateman attended several colleges throughout his training *(including studying Theology at Roffey Place, Horsham, UK and a Member of Kerygma - with Rev. Colin Urquhart and Dr. Bob Gordon - 1985-1987)* before being awarded a Doctorate of Divinity *(2006)* in recognition of his lifetime achievements by the International College of Excellence, now "DanEl Christian College" *(President: Dr. Robb Thompson USA)* also "Life Christian University" *(Dr. Douglas Wingate USA)* where he also earned a Bachelor of Theology B.Th. *(2006),* a Master of Arts in Theology M.A., a Doctor of Ministry in Theology D.Min., *(2007)* and Doctor of Philosophy in Theology Ph.D. *(2013)* from LICU.

❖

To Contact the Author

Please email:

Alan Pateman Ministries International

Email: apostledr@alanpateman.com
Web: www.AlanPatemanMinistries.com

*Please include your prayer requests
and comments when you write.*

❖

Other Books

Media, Spiritual Gateway

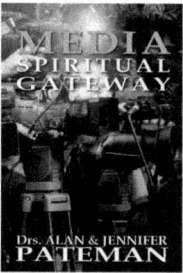

Let's face it; we live in the era of fake news! It's always existed, but never been quite so prominent. Today it's an all-out-war between fact and political fiction.

ISBN: 978-1-909132-54-2, Pages: 192,
Format: Paperback, Published: 2018
Also available in eBook format!

Millennial Myopia, From a Biblical Perspective

The standard for every generation is Jesus. However Millennial Myopia describes the trap of focusing everything on one particular generation or demographic cohort, at the exclusion and expense of all others. The Church cannot afford to make this mistake too.

ISBN: 978-1-909132-67-2, Pages: 216,
Format: Paperback, Published: 2017
Also available in eBook format!

Truth for the Journey Books

TONGUES, Our Supernatural Prayer Language

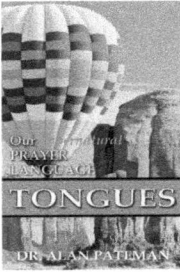

In writing to the church at Corinth, Paul encouraged them to continue the practice of speaking with other tongues in their worship of God and in their prayer lives as a means of spiritual edification. "He that speaketh in an unknown tongue edifies, charges, builds himself up like a battery."

ISBN: 978-1-909132-44-3, Pages: 144,
Format: Paperback, Published: 2016
Also available in eBook format!

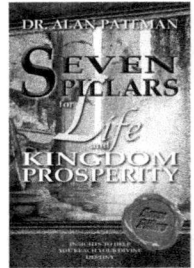

Seven Pillars for Life and Kingdom Prosperity

I submit these "Seven Pillars for Life and Kingdom Prosperity" to you, (Love, Prayer, Righteousness, Obedience, Connections, Management, Money). It's my desire that you walk in the triumphs that God has ordained for you.

ISBN: 978-1-909132-46-7, Pages: 220,
Format: Paperback, Published: 2016
Also available in eBook format!

Seduction & Control: Infiltrating Society & the Church

This book is a glance into the world of seduction and control, how they try to influence the Church through many powerful avenues such as the New Age, sexual education in our schools, basic entertainment; things that touch our everyday lives in order that we effectively and gradually become desensitised.

ISBN: 978-1-909132-00-9, Pages: 156
Format: Paperback, Published: 2015
Also available in eBook format!

Truth for the Journey Books

Kingdom Management for Anointed Prosperity

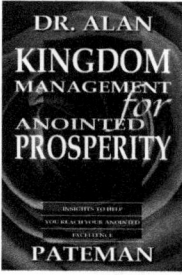

In his book, "Kingdom Management for Anointed Prosperity," Dr. Alan Pateman reveals how we can avoid living in continual crisis due to mismanagement. Life happens to all of us, but how we handle it matters most.

ISBN: 978-1-909132-34-4, Pages: 144, Format: Paperback, Published: 2015
Also available in eBook format!

Why War: A Biblical Approach to the Armour of God and Spiritual Warfare

Spiritual warfare means different things to different people, but from a biblical standpoint Ephesians 6:10-18 gives us the best biblical definition of spiritual warfare possible. We can also see how God has thoroughly equipped us for victory not just self defence!

ISBN: 978-1-909132-39-9, Pages: 180, Format: Paperback, Published: 2013
Also available in eBook format!

Forgiveness, The Key to Revival

Scripture is absolute when it comes to forgiveness. IF we forgive, THEN we are forgiven. It's that simple but no one said it was easy! Nonetheless, forgiveness can be likened to a spiritual key that unlocks spiritual doors and opportunities!

ISBN: 978-1-909132-41-2, Pages: 124, Format: Paperback, Published: 2013
Also available in eBook format!

Truth for the Journey Books

Revival Fires - Anointed Generals
Past & Present (Part Two of Four)

Seasons might be changing but God's Word remains the same. The heart of the author is to help train, equip and be a blessing to those men and women who will be willing to fulfil their potential in ministry and be properly equipped for service.

ISBN: 978-1-909132-36-8, Pages: 142,
Format: Paperback, Published: 2012
Also available in eBook format!

Prayer, Touching the Heart of God (Part Two)

Touching the Heart of God is the very essence of prayer. Whether we are petitioning God with very specific requests or consecrating ourselves before Him and rededicating our lives - whatever the case may be – the true essence of all praying is "Touching the Heart of God."

ISBN: 978-1-909132-12-2, Pages: 180,
Format: Paperback, Published: 2012
Also available in eBook format!

Prayer, Ingredients for Successful Intercession
(Part One)

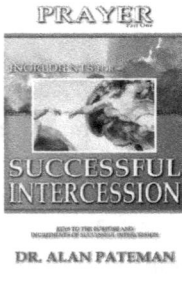

This Book is the first of two books on Prayer. Dr. Pateman provides an exhaustive study, showcasing the vital ingredients necessary for all successful prayer. An excellent power-packed teaching tool, either for the individual or for the local church prayer group, that's eager to lay a solid foundation but don't know where to start!

ISBN: 978-1-909132-11-5, Pages: 140,
Format: Paperback, Published: 2012
Also available in eBook format!

Truth for the Journey Books

Apostles: Can the Church Survive Without Them?

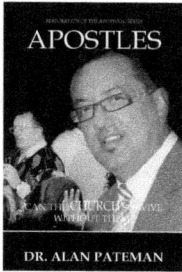

Before Jesus returns a significant increase of the anointing will be poured out on the Body of Christ, but can the Church handle such an anointing? *(Acts 5:5)* Billy Brim once said, "As much as the anointing is powerful to create, it is as powerfully destructive of evil." The fear of God will be restored with the apostolic and people will begin walking with such anointing, as we have never seen before!

ISBN: 978-1-909132-04-7, Pages: 164,
Format: Paperback, Published: 2012
Also available in eBook format!

Sexual Madness: In a Sexually Confused World

This book discusses the sensitive subject of political correctness in our world today and the growing fear of causing offence in the public arena. It also discusses the rise of homosexuality, pedophilia and all other forms of sexuality, as there are many. Including modern statistics on pornography.

ISBN: 978-1-909132-02-3, Pages: 160,
Format: Paperback, Published: 2012
Also available in eBook format!

His Life is in the Blood

Blood is the trophy of every battle. The spilt blood of Jesus Christ is our trophy. It is our freedom from sin and bondage. Nothing can enter the blood-bought temples of the Holy Ghost! This book will encourage you to apply the blood of Jesus our Passover Lamb to your life, just as the children of Israel did in the Old Testament. Not merely talking or reading about it, but applying it.

ISBN: 978-1-909132-06-1, Pages: 152,
Format: Paperback, First Published: 2007
Also available in eBook format!

Dear Friends,

Have you considered becoming one of our international students? We are privileged to welcome you, from around the world, to "LifeStyle International Christian University" *(the teaching arm of Alan Pateman Ministries International).* **An English speaking university** dedicated to your success; to see you trained and equipped to fully succeed in your God given Destiny.

It is our passion to raise up the leaders of tomorrow, who will have influence in all realms of authority, including the Body of Christ. Men and women of strategy, wisdom and true godliness, who'll stand with stature and maturity in this hour.

It's undeniable that in today's world, recognised education has become indispensable, therefore it is our desire to offer well balanced and well structured courses. Those that have been written by gifted and talented ministers of God, who seek to be inspired by God's Holy Spirit.

Consequently we have put together a **flexible curriculum,** designed both for correspondence students and campuses, which is a strategy to reach the distant learner; whether provincial, national or international. In fact we have many correspondence students from around the world, including a growing number of successful campuses, in various countries.

This is a growing platform, where men and women of dignity and passion, can grow and be established in their God given endeavours. As God is the healer of the nations, we pray and believe that many of our alumni will go on to **become world changers** in their own right.

We are proud of each and every one of our LICU students.

It would be our pleasure if you would join them on this incredible journey!

Doctor Alan Pateman

Alan Pateman Prof. Ph.D., D.Min., D.D., M.A., B.Th.
PRESIDENT AND CEO
www.licuuniversity.com www.cfeapostolicnetwork.com
Email: info@licuuniversity.com Mob: +39 366 329 1315

For more information visit our website/facebook or contact our office, using the details below:

Website: www.licuuniversity.com
Facebook: www.facebook.com/LICUMainCampus
Email: info@licuuniversity.com
Telephone: +39 366 329 1315

ALAN PATEMAN MINISTRIES
PRESENTS

TEACHING - LEARNING - LIVING
A MASTER CLASS
with Dr Alan Pateman

DR. ALAN IS AVAILABLE
TO HOLD TEACHING
SEMINARS ON SATURDAYS
WITH YOUR LEADERS /
MEMBERS AND THEN
MINISTER AT YOUR
SUNDAY SERVICE.
PLEASE CONTACT OUR
OFFICE FOR AVAILABILITY.

OFFICE: VIA DEL GALLO, 18,
55100 LUCCA (LU), ITALY
TEL. 0039 366 329 1315
APOSTLEDR@ALANPATEMAN.COM

www.alanpatemanministries.com